Financial Management and Investment Decisions

FINANCIAL MANAGEMENT AND INVESTMENT DECISIONS

By

Jagmohan Negi

Formerly

Director - Professor,

Amity School of Hospitality

and

Gaurav Manoher J.

UNIVERSITY SCIENCE PRESS

(An Imprint of Laxmi Publications Pvt. Ltd.)

BANGALORE • CHENNAI • COCHIN • GUWAHATI • HYDERABAD
JALANDHAR • KOLKATA • LUCKNOW • MUMBAI • PATNA
RANCHI • NEW DELHI

Published by
UNIVERSITY SCIENCE PRESS
(*An Imprint of Laxmi Publications Pvt. Ltd.*)
113, Golden House, Daryaganj,
New Delhi-110002
Phone : 011-43 53 25 00
Fax : 011-43 53 25 28
www.laxmipublications.com
info@laxmipublications.com

First Edition: 2012

OFFICES

✆ **Bangalore**	080-26 75 69 30	✆ **Chennai**	044-24 34 47 26
✆ **Cochin**	0484-237 70 04, 405 13 03	✆ **Guwahati**	0361-251 36 69, 251 38 81
✆ **Hyderabad**	040-24 65 23 33	✆ **Jalandhar**	0181-222 12 72
✆ **Kolkata**	033-22 27 43 84	✆ **Lucknow**	0522-220 99 16
✆ **Mumbai**	022-24 91 54 15, 24 92 78 69	✆ **Patna**	0612-230 00 97
✆ **Ranchi**	0651-221 47 64		

UFM-9641-150-FIN MGMT & INVEST DEC-NEG C—

Typeset at: Sukuvisa Enterprises, New Delhi. *Printed at*:

CONTENTS

PREFACE

In finance our goal is to create wealth. We learn from experience how to cope with routine problems. The most successful are those who are able to respond to change. To do so we need more than time-honored rules of thumb; we must understand why companies and financial markets behave the way they do. In other words, we need a theory and principles of finance.

Much of this book is concerned with understanding what financial managers do and why. But we also say what financial managers should do to increase company value.

The book provides an introduction to these burning topics in the field of finance. We begin introduction to finance, where we introduce you to financial planning, financial control, profit maximization analysis, functions of finance, the basic tools of finance and decision-making. We present the decision-making which includes capital budgeting, capital structure and the management of working capital

We have also put more emphasis on financial planning and the management of working capital. For example, the discussion of financial statements and ratios and common-size balance sheets and income statements.

The book helps you to grasp what is going on in the world around you. It helps you to ask the right questions when times change and new problems need to be analyzed. It also tells you which things you do not need to worry about. Throughout this book we show how managers use financial principles to solve practical problems.

The book develops new themes and ideas. Over the years the literature on finance has focused more on understanding what financial managers do and the reasons for their actions. In other words, finance has become more positive and less normative. For example, in recent years there have been a number of useful surveys of firms' capital investment practices, payout policies, decisions to go public, and their choice of capital structure. We review these surveys and look at how they cast light on competing theories.

We recognize the financial managers, increasingly work in an international environment and therefore need to be familiar with differences in institutional structure and corporate practice. We hope that this material will provide a better understanding of the wider financial environment and be useful to our many readers around the world.

We realize that instructors will wish to select from these topics and many will prefer a different sequence. Therefore, we have ensured that the text is modular, so that topics can be introduced in several logical orders. For example, there should be no difficulty in reading the material on financial statement analysis and short-term financial decisions before the chapters on capital investment.

The book devotes special chapters to dividend policy and to share repurchases as an alternative to dividend payouts. The dividend decision, incorporate finance, is a decision made by the directors of a company. It relates to the amount and timing of any cash payments made to the company's stockholders. The decision is an important one for the corporate as it may influence its capital structure and stock price. In addition, the decision may determine the amount of taxation that stockholders pay. There are three main factors that may influence a firm's dividend decision:

- Free-cash flow
- Dividend clienteles
- Information signaling.

Under this theory, the dividend decision is very simple. The corporate simply pays out, as dividends, any cash that is surplus after it invests in all available positive net present value projects.

The dividend decision is usually taken by considering at least the three questions of: How much excess cash is available? What do our investors prefer?, and What will be the effect on our stock price of announcing the amount of the dividend?

When investors have incomplete information about the firm, perhaps due to opaque accounting practices, they will look for other information that may provide a clue as to the firm's future prospects. Managers have more information than investors about the firm, and such information may affect their dividend decisions. When managers lack confidence in the firm's ability to generate cash flows in the future they may keep dividends constant, or possibly even reduce the amount of dividends paid out. Conversely, managers that have access to information that indicates very good future prospects are more likely to increase dividends.

The goal of the text is not merely to teach the tools of a discipline or trade but also to enable the readers to abstract what is learned to new and yet unforeseen problems – in short, to educate the readers in finance.

The book is written for students of financial management. For many readers it is their first look at the world of finance. Therefore, we try to make the book simpler, clearer, and more fun to read. But the book is also used extensively as a reference and guide for practicing managers around the world. Therefore, we strive to make it more comprehensive and authoritative. We believe that this publication is better for both the students and the practicing managers.

This book provides the readers with conceptual understanding of financial making process, rather than just an introduction to the tools and techniques of finance. Practical Illustration are incorporated for easy understanding of the readers.

The book is intended for students, and managers with requisite knowledge in economics, accounting, and statistics.

The book includes its own recommended readings list. Important terms and a list of acronyms used in the text are included at the end of the book.

—Authors

ACKNOWLEDGEMENT

We gratefully acknowledge the assistance, support, and encouragement of those individuals who have contributed to the preparation of Financial Management and Investment Decisions. Specifically, we wish to recognize the very helpful insights provided by many our colleagues, for their careful comments and helpful reviews of the text.

We express our sincere thanks to those using Financial Management and Investment Decisions in classrooms. We thank you for making us a part of your team. Always feel free to give any of us a call or contact us through the Internet when you have questions or needs.

—Authors

List of Figures and Tables

List of Tables

List of Figures

Chapter 1

FINANCE AND BUSINESS DEVELOPMENT

Finance is one of the most important business function but in recent times due to various developments such as increasing number of business units and their scales of operation, changing structure of economy, globalization of economy, rising price levels, and the increasing importance of the government in its use of financial resources, the finance as a business function, is gaining an importance and a distinctive status.

In the initial stage, the accounting function was regarded not very different from financial function. This was primarily due to the fact that terms and concepts used in both are identical and similar. Accounting is essentially a sequence concerned with data gathering, classifying and recording them in a specified manner while financial management is concerned with the analysis of the data for the purpose of decision making.

Finance is the life-blood of business and is the key determinant of the success of all other business functions. It is the lubricant of the process of economic growth. "Something must direct the flow of economic activity and facilitate its smooth operation. Finance is the agent that produces this result." (Ref.: Husband and Dockery in Modern Corporation Finance).

"Finance may be defined as that administrative area or set of administrative functions in an organization which relates to arrangement of cash and credit so that the organization may have means to carry out its objectives as satisfactorily as possible." (Ref.: Howard and Uptron: Introduction to Business Finance).

Business finance can broadly be defined as the activity concerned with planning, raising, controlling and administering of funds used in business (Ref.: Guthman and Duggal). Finance in general terms may be defined as the study of money– its nature, creation, behaviour, regulation and problems. It is concerned with the ways in which businessmen, investors, governments financial institutions and families deal with funds or money.

Traditionally, corporation finance was the term used for financial management. In essence, it implies financing the corporate enterprise *i.e.,* procurement of funds. In fact, this approach ignored the allocation or utilization of funds. It is now recognized that efficient performance of finance function requires the application of general principles of management. Though, it is very difficult to enumerate all the functions performed by management, yet the most important aspects of financial management are:

1. Planning
2. Organizing, and
3. Control.

FINANCIAL PLANNING

Basically planning is selling out the future activities of business in financial terms. In the words of Koontz and O' Donnel, "Planning is the executive function which involves one selection from among alternatives of enterprise objectives, procedures, policies and programmes."

To be more cogent, planning is deciding in advance what is to be done, *i.e.*, " Plan is projected course of action."

It includes:

1. Establishing the firm's objectives.
2. Determining firms' policies.
3. Establishing procedures which must be followed to achieve goals. In technical terms, financial planning included determination of financial goals, economics of acquisition of money quantity and quality and optimum use of funds.

Steps in Financial Planning

STEP 1. Selling up of the Goals and Objectives:

As stated earlier the first step in financial planning is the **setting up of the goals or objectives**– usually to employ capital in whatever proportion necessary to yield maximum productivity from each factor of production over the long run. In dynamic society economic condition change and to take advantage of changing economic situation or environment, firm should establish long and short-term goals. The long-term goals is to use capital in appropriate proportion to aim at the maximum possible profitability of the enterprise. The long-term goals is to be so designed that it does not jeopardize the short-term goal of solvency for survival.

STEP 2. Formulation of Policies:

The second step is the formulation of policies dealing with procurement, disbursement and administration of funds. To be more specific these are:

1. Policies governing the amount of capital required for the firm keeping in view the objectives
2. Policies determining the owners vs. lenders share in the capital
3. Policies governing credit and collection activities of the firm
4. Policies regarding income determination and distribution.

STEP 3. Formulation of Procedures:

The third step is the formulation of the procedures. Procedures imply a series of steps and each step is called a method. Procedures would help each individual know what he has to do.

STEP 4. Provision of Flexibility:

The last step is to provide flexibility so that administration becomes easy.

Limitation of Financial Planning

Some of the main limitation of financial planning are:

1. Planning is a blue print of future course of action which requires facts about future. Facts about future are non-existent. As such assumption about future must be substituted by suitable forecasts–purchases, sales, operations etc.
2. Reluctance or inability of management to change plans.
3. Lack of coordination or indecision among personnel.

Financial Organization

Organizing function is normally concerned with functional determination, allocation and delegation. Three things are of great relevance in deciding the nature of financial organization:

1. Size of the enterprise
2. Nature of the enterprise
3. Capacity, experience and interest of the finance man to be used for the purpose.

Keeping in view the above factors financial organization would be concerned with:

1. Identifying all financial activities and their division
2. Determination of financial activities to be performed by line and top and staff personnel
3. Deciding about channels of reporting and the persons incharge
4. How to affect coordination among different activities?

Precisely speaking financial organization is concerned with grouping of financial activities in operational terms and delegation of sufficient authority to the operating levels.

Financial Control

If the organization has to achieve the goals set under planning process, it must exercise control function very effectively. Control function is composed of four important phases:

1. Determination of operational standards of performance
2. Measurement of actual performance and its evaluation in relation to pre-determined goals
3. Determination of deviation and corrective action
4. Development of standards for performance evaluation.

Traditionally, the so called 'Munim ji', the financial manager, was engaged in record keeping, preparation of accounts and managing cash whenever business needed it. For a considerable period of time financial management was viewed as an activity mainly concerned with raising of funds.

Gradually, the nature of finance function has changed considerably. As business becomes more complex, finance function assumed the role which far exceeded the traditional role of preparing reports and rasing funds. Today's Financial Manager deals with issues affecting liquidity and profitability. He deals with:

1. Financing risk and costs
2. Diversification of activity, *i.e.*, new produce development, new market and new business
3. Rate of inflation and its impact on business

4. Uses of funds
5. Changing technology and need for expenditure on research and development
6. Speedy dissemination of information.

Today, finance function has become most exciting, complex and challenging. It is now concerned with solving the following problems:

1. Which new proposals for investment be accepted?
2. What steps be taken to increase the market value of shares?
3. How much working capital be employed to support operations?
4. Should it declare dividends?
5. If so how much?

Thus, it is quite clear that finance is concerned with managing flows of money, *i.e.*, inflows and outflows of money.

The major decisions in the field of finance are broadly categorized as:

1. *Financing decision, i.e.*, determining capital structure.
2. *Investment decision, i.e.*, how much funds to be committed to long-term assets like building, plant and machinery etc. (This is technically called capital expenditure decision or capital budgeting decision) and how to manage short-term assets like stock, debtors cash etc. (This is technically called working capital management).
3. *Dividend decision*: It is concerned with deciding the amount of profits to be distributed as dividends to shareholders and the amount to be retained for financing growth. (Each of these decision will be discussed in details).

Objectives of Financial Management

A clear cut definition of objectives of business and that of each of its major activities provides a frame work for optimum financial decision-making. In our context we are attempting to identify the goal, the financial management must set before itself while taking decision regarding financing, investment and dividend. There are two approaches to define objectives of financial management.

1. How to raise long-term funds and what will be the cost?

   (This aspect will be dealt in *Chapter 2. Long-term Finance and Capital Structure*)
2. Maximization of profit.

MAXIMIZATION OF PROFITS

The maximization of profits is considered to be a goal of financial management. The advocates of this approach argue that profits serve as a true test of economic efficiency of operations. It helps us in measuring and comparing economic performance of management. Further, it is profit that leads to the optimum allocation of resources among competing activities and under conditions of perfect competition, it leads to the optimum economic results through the operation of price-mechanism.

Although profit maximization is an important objective of financial management, it has come under severe criticism in the recent literature. Ezra Solomon rejects this approach on three grounds:

1. The concept of profit is vague. It is very difficult to exactly understand what profit means. Should it be gross profit or net profit, total profit or rate of profit, short-term profit or long-term profit?
2. It ignores the timing of inflow. It is a matter of common knowledge that money received today has a higher value than received in future. Thus, if a firm is maximizing profits, should it accept 20% return for three years or 18% for five years.
3. This concept overlooks the quality of future benefits.

The quality of future returns is said to be better if the variations in inflow are the minimum. Thus, between two projects say *A* and *B*, if *A* brings ₹ 90,000, ₹ 1,00,000 and ₹ 1,10,000 during periods of recession, normal and inflation as against project '*B*' which brings ₹ 1,10,000 during normal period and gives ₹ 2,00,000 during inflation but yields zero during recession, project '*A*' is decidedly better because it is more consistent. Profit maximization objective ignores this distinction.

Prof. Solomon recommends that as an alternative **wealth maximization** is better operational goal because it is based on cash flows rather than profits. Cash flow is a concise and clear term. It hardly lacks precision.

Wealth maximization takes into account quality as well as quantity of benefits. It follows bigger and the better principles and at the same time takes into account the time value of money. It would be appropriate to quote Ezra Solomon who describes wealth maximization objectives as:

"The gross present worth of a course of action is equal to the capitalized value of the flow of future expected benefits discounted at a rate which reflects their certainty or uncertainty. Any financial action which creates wealth or which has a net present worth above zero is a desirable one and should be undertaken. If two or more desirable courses of action are mutually exclusive (if any one can be undertaken) then the decision should be to do that which creates most wealth or shows the greatest amount of net present worth. In short, the operating objective for financial management is to maximize wealth or net present worth. (*Ref. Ezra, Solomon: The Theory of Financial Management, 1969, p.20.*)

Thus the wealth maximization objective automatically incorporates the time value of money and quality of returns and risk associated with a project. It does by choosing an appropriate rate of discount and using this rate to find out net present worth of future benefits by discounting the future stream of benefits by this rate.

A firm that is maximizing its shareholders' wealth must do the following:

1. **Avoid high level of risk:**

   Projects that carry a high degree of risk, though undoubtedly with a high rate of return, are not to be accepted because a single failure would jeopardize its continued existence.

2. **Pay regular dividends:**

   Dividends constitute payment out of present or past profits to the equity owners. A firm attempting to maximize its shareholders wealth must pay dividends. In the earlier years of growth, it may pay less and retain more but after a particular period, it may pay more when its cash needs are not big or its self generated funds are larger.

3. **Seek growth:**

   Management must look for increase in sales and earnings with a view to maximizing its wealth. A large, stable and diversified volume of sales provide cushion for unforeseen recessionary trends.

4. **Maintain market price of its stock/shares:**

   Management must maintain the market price of its stocks by explaining its own action to generate confidence in the investors.

FUNCTIONS OF FINANCIAL MANAGEMENT

Functions of financial management can be classified into two sets:

1. One related to the twin goals of liquidity and profitability, and
2. Second related to what is being managed, assets or funds.

In the second case it performs dual role – one as a decision-maker and two as an adviser.

1. Functions Leading to Liquidity

(*i*) Forecasting cash flows and matching of inflows and outflows.

(*ii*) Raising funds–selection between various sources – shares debentures, term loans, public deposits, retained earnings, bank loan, leasing etc., as well as proper timing of their issue.

(*iii*) Managing the flow of internal funds. Coordination between where funds are idle and where they are needed.

2. Functions Leading to Profitability

(*i*) **Cost control:**

Coordination between costing and accounting function. Measuring the amount of money to be spent. Identifying cost of raising funds.

(*ii*) **Pricing:**

It is a critical element in company's marketing effort, image and level of sales. Finance Manager and Marketing Manager has to take a decision with regard to pricing of its goods and services.

(*iii*) **Forecasting future profits:**

Must gather and analyse data and make forecast about future levels of profits. It would help in financial planning.

(*iv*) **Measuring cost of capital:**

Equity and debt capital costs are different. Estimate both and determine the profit necessary to pay off all interest on borrowed funds and the borrowed funds themselves.

(*v*) **Managing assets:**

Determine the mix of the assets required to run the business. Effective utilization of business assets and reducing waste. Converting idle equipments to cash improves liquidity. Reducing cost improves profitability.

(*vi*) **Managing funds:**

The finance manager acts as a specialized staff. He is responsible for advising the top man so as to have sufficient funds to finance receivables, inventories and cash availability to pay dividends etc.

Goals and functions of Financial Management can be shown in Fig. 1.1.

Profit Maximization

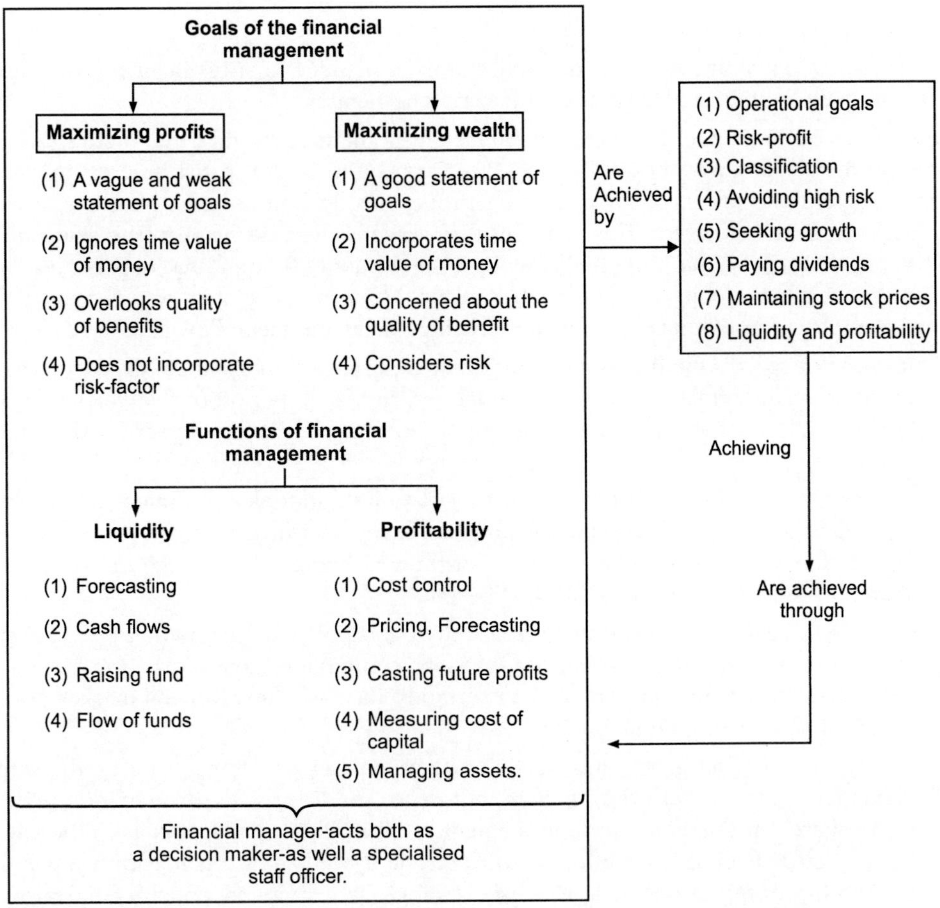

Fig. 1.1 Profit vs Wealth maximization as objectives of financial management

Illustration 1.1

Differentiate between the profit maximization and the wealth maximization objectives of financial management.

Solution:

Difference between Profit Maximization and Value Maximization

The two most important objectives of financial management are as follows:

1. Profit maximization
2. Value maximization.

1. *Objective of profit maximization*:

Under this objective the financial manager's sole objective is to maximize profits. The objective could be short-term or long-term. Under the short-term objective the manager would intend to show profitability in a short run, say one year. When profit maximization becomes a long-term objective the concern of the financial manager is to manage finances in such a way so as to maximize the EPS of the company.

2. ***Objective of value maximization:***

Under this objective the financial manager strives to manage finances in such a way so as to continuously increase the market price of the companies shares.

Under the short-term profit maximization objective a manager could continue to show profit increases by merely issuing stock and using the proceeds to invest in risk free or near to risk free securities. He may also opt for increasing profits through other non-operational activities like disposal of fixed assets etc. This shall result in a consistent decrease in the share holders profit– that is earning per share shall fall. Hence it is commonly thought that maximizing profits in the long run is a better objective. This shall increase the earning per share on a consistent basis. However even this objective has its own shortcomings, which are as follows:

1. It does not specify the timing or duration of expected returns, hence one cannot be sure whether an investment fetching a ₹ 10 lac return after a period of five years is more or less valuable than an investment fetching a return of ₹ 1.5 lac per year for the next five years.
2. It does not consider the risk factor of project to be undertaken, in many cases a highly levered firm may have the same earnings per share as a firm having a lesser percentage of debt in the capital structure. In spite of the EPS being the same the market price per share of the two companies shall be different.
3. This objective does not allow the effect of dividend policy on the market price per share, in order to maximize the earning per share the companies may not pay any dividend. In such cases the earning per share shall certainly increase, however the market price per share could as well go down.

   For the reasons just given, an objective of maximizing profits may not be the same as maximizing the market price of share and hence the firms value. The market price of a firm's share represents the focal judgement of all market participants as to the value of the particular firm. It takes into account present as well as futuristic earnings per share; the timing, duration and risk of these earnings; the dividend policy of the firm; and other factors that bear upon the market price of the share. The market price serves as a barometer of the company's performance; it indicates how well management is doing on behalf of is shareholders. Management is under continuous watch. Shareholders who are not satisfied may sell their shares and invest in some other company. This action, if taken, will put downward pressure on the market price per share and hence reduce the company's value.

FIELDS OF FINANCE

Finance is related to diverse fields some of which are:

1. **Public finance:**

   Central, state and local governments handle large sum of money. Money is used in accordance with policies and procedures. Business try to make profits but government will attempt to accomplish social objectives.

2. **Securities and investment analysis:**

   Purchase of shares, debentures and other securities involves analysis and techniques that are highly specialized. An investor has to measure the risk, and probable performance. It involves the trade off between risk and returns.

3. **International finance:**

   Each country has its own currency. Conversion from one to other is required. When money crosses the international boundaries – it involves special type of problems, such as balance of payment problems and inflation. The study of flows of funds between individual and organization across national borders and development of methods to handle the flow efficiently is within the scope of international finance.

4. **Institutional finance:**

   Banks, Insurance, term lending institutions.

   Institutional finance deals with issues of capital formation and organizations performing financing function.

5. **Financial management:**

   Individual business face problems dealing with the acquisition of funds and optimum methods of employing funds.

Relation with Other Functional Areas

1. **Economics:**

   Economics is concerned with analyzing the distribution of resources in a society. It is interested in demand and supply, costs and profits, production and consumption.

2. **Macro-Economics:**

   Studies overall economic situation of a nation or group of nations. It is concerned with gross national product to measure the growth of economy.

3. **Micro-Economics:**

   Studies the way business firm makes decisions about pricing and production.

   The field of finance rests heavily on the work of economists. It is closely related to micro-economics, economics forecasts, economics forecasts for the industry, finance forecasts for the firm, finance uses and macro-economics models.

REVIEW QUESTIONS

1. (*a*) Explain the meaning of the term 'finance'.

   (*b*) What are the different fields of finance?

   (*c*) How is finance related with economics?

2. "Wealth maximization is a better operational goal than profit maximization". Comment.

3. Enumerate briefly the functions of financial management.

Chapter 2

LONG-TERM FINANCE AND CAPITAL STRUCTURE

Along with a carefully prepared feasibility study, the method of financing and operation is one of the key areas in determining the viability of a new hotel project. We have chosen to link the method of operation, in the sense of financial arrangements, with that of financing, as this may influence both the level of risk and the prospective profitability.

There is no easy answer to the problem of how to select a method of financing for a project and many different approaches are used. The great danger to avoid is overcapitalization. If too much money is tied up in the project; it increases the charges for capital that the unit has to bear, while at the same time raising the level of profits that need to be earned so as to provide a reasonable rate of return. Overcapitalised businesses are associated with buildings that are too big or too expensively designed, low utilization of plant because too much has been installed, large inventory holdings as a result of poor management and planning, heavy customer debts through weak credit procedures and cash surpluses that are not earning interest because cash flow is not controlled.

MINIMIZING CAPITAL REQUIREMENTS

Undercapitalization is not so serious a problem as many methods are available to provide temporary increase in funds. Policies that might be adopted to reduce the capital requirements of a project include:

1. *Premises*—Rent the premises instead of buying or, if owned, sell and lease back.
2. *Equipment*—Equipment can be leased or bought on hire purchase.

   Minimal equipment inventories can be supplemented as required by renting.
3. *Stocks*—Overinvestment can be prevented by careful planning and control or by changing the service system. Production of some items can be subcontracted (which also reduces the need for equipment and space) or purchased so as to minimize waste. Small batch sizes or foods with longer storage life (frozen or chilled) will achieve this.

4. *Debts*—A good credit control system will prevent debt becoming too large. Techniques such as discount for prompt payment, or the factoring of debt, may also be used.
5. *Credit*—Use all the credit consistent with good relations with suppliers. Cash management procedures should aim to balance the flow of payables with receivables.

A review of these points will suggest that a wide range of policies are available to any business. The method chosen will reflect the objectives and form of the organization, (some techniques are not equally possible for all types of business), the current environment (particularly that created by government fiscal policies) and the planned life of the investment. It will also depend on attitudes to risk. Some people hold to the view that it is better to own things that increase in value (buildings) and rent or lease those which decline (most operating equipment). On the other hand there are unhappy investing in a business that does not seem to own a substantial proportion of the fixed assets which it uses and do not like companies that engage in 'off-balance-sheet financing techniques', they feel perhaps that if the business fails then there will be nothing substantial to sell which will cover their investment.

Undercapitalisation also has its dangers. The equipment leases may prove much more expensive than purchasing. Discounts may be lost due to lack of liquid (cash) resources. Therefore, follow the general rule to minimize capital investment and to test each decision to increase the level of capital by comparing the costs with the amount of extra profit that will be generated. It is the use of assets not their ownership which will earn money.

A business house may decide to use a financial mix consisting of different types of financial securities. (A financial security is a legal instrument that represents either an ownership or a creditorship claim on company). Two basic kinds of securities are of concern to the financial manager are:

1. Equity securities or ownership securities *i.e.,* equity shares
2. Debt securities, *i.e.,* debentures, mortgages, long-term debt, public deposits or funds raised from term-lending institutions.

LONG-TERMS FINANCE

There are two principal sources of long-term finance:

1. Share capital: issues of shares
2. Long-term loans: debentures and mortgages.

Shares Capital

The issuing of shares is only possible in large companies. Although there is no legal obstacle to any company which would like to issue shares it will be unable to obtain a market quotation unless it satisfies the rules of the Stock Exchange on which they are to be sold. For most purposes stocks and shares are the same. However, stocks must always be fully paid and may be purchased in fractional amounts. Neither of these conditions apply to shares. These rules specify a minimum valuation for the company, a minimum valuation of each class of share and minimum percentage of public ownership. Brokers and issuing houses are also likely to have some influence and it would be unusual for a new public company's market valuation to be less than the prescribed limit.

The planning of a share issue is a marketing operation in itself. The shares may be offered for sale in a variety of ways: at a fixed price, by tender, by subscription (prospectus), by public placing, or at a special cut price to existing shareholders (a rights issue). In the case of an existing company the price will be related to the current market price of its shares and its current trading performance.

If the shares are priced too high, they may not all be sold. The protect itself against this possibility the company can use a underwriter, who for a fee, will guarantee to buy all unsold shares.

On the other hand, if the shares are priced too high, they may not all be sold. To protect itself against this after sale the company has lost additional potential capital. This might be avoided by forecasting capital needs well in advance so that the issue can be made when the market is healthy, and by choosing an issuing house (stockbroker or merchant bank) with care examine part performance in detail and ensure the best advice.

Two types of share may be issued.

1. Equity shares
2. Preference shares.

Equity Shares

Equity shares enable the holder to participate in that portion of the company's surplus profits which the directors decide to pay out, after meeting the interest on loan capital and preference shares; thus they participate fully in the risk and it is therefore expected that the return will correspond to that. Equity shareholders have the right to vote at company meetings.

The rights and responsibilities attaching to equity consists of positive considerations/income potential and control of the firm and negative considerations–loss potential, legal responsibility and personal liability.

Equity Enjoys two Types of Rights

1. Collective Rights

(*i*) To amend the charter *i.e.*, Memorandum of Association

(*ii*) To adopt and amend by-laws *i.e.*, Articles of Association

(*iii*) To elect the directors of the corporation

(*iv*) To authorize the sale of fixed Assets

(*v*) To enter into mergers

(*vi*) To change the amount of authorised capital

(*vii*) To issue preference shares, debentures, and other securities.

2. Specific Rights

(*i*) Right to vote

(*ii*) To sell or transfer ownership interest to other persons

(*iii*) To inspect the books of the company

(*iv*) Right to share the assets on liquidation.

Positive Considerations

The important positive considerations involved in equity ownership are:

1. Income and Control

The right to income carries a risk of loss as well. And control involves liability and responsibility.

2. Apportionment of Control

The legal control of the corporation vests in the hands of equity owners. However this is a debatable issue since in practice the oligarchic character prevails, *i.e.*, the control by a few.

3. Apportionment of Risk

The highest degree of risk is attached with the equity since they are the last in the priority of claims at the time of liquidation. The portion of capital they contribute, provides a cushion for creditors if losses occur on dissolution. The equity to total assets ratio indicates the percentage by which assets may shrink in value on liquidation before creditors will incur losses.

4. Evaluation of Common Stock/Equity as a Source of Funds

From the corporate's is point of view the attractions of equity issue are:

(*i*) It does not entail fixed charge. Equity dividends can be paid only if the company generates earnings. There is no legal obligation to pay dividends to the equity owners even it there are profits.

(*ii*) It carries no fixed maturity dates.

(*iii*) The sale of equity increase the credit-worthiness of the firm as it provides cushion against losses for the creditors.

(*iv*) Common stock may be easily sold as it appeals to a particular type of investors for two reasons:

  (*a*) It carries a higher expected return than preference shares

  (*b*) It increases in value when the assets of the corporation appreciate for any reason.

5. From the Social Point of View

(*i*) It is claimed that the equity financing tends to stabilize the economy since it involves no fixed charges if sales and earnings decline.

(*ii*) In other forms of financing the fixed charges may force the firm to bankruptcy in the event of inadequacy of profits to pay fixed obligations.

Disadvantages of Common Stock

(*i*) Use of equity extends control to new entrance. The management may not desire to share control.

(*ii*) Use of common stock gives the right to share profit.

(*iii*) Cost of underwriting and distribution is higher in case of equity than other securities.

(*iv*) In the absence of desirable levels of debt, the cost of capital will be higher.

(*v*) Equity dividends are not deductible as an expense for calculating income while debenture interest is deductible which brings down their real cost considerably.

Preferred Stock

Preference shares combine the features of both debt and common stock.

Preference shares are somewhat of a rarity now-a-days. In effect money is obtained from preference shareholders much in the form of an unsecured loan and to compensate for this they are given priority rights to dividend payment and capital repayment. The preference shareholders have no voting rights and dividends are not deductible in arriving at taxable profits, whereas loan and debenture interest are.

Features of Preference Shares as a Source of Funds

1. Preference to Dividends
2. Preference to Assets
3. Basically a fixed return
4. Indefinite life with a call feature
5. Usually non-voting
6. Cumulative Dividends
7. Convertible Clause.

Advantages

Gordon Donaldson has strongly defended the use of preferred stock as means of financing. He suggests that from the stand point of the company's share holders the priority list of financing may be:

(*i*) Debt

(*ii*) Preferred stock

(*iii*) Retained earnings

(*iv*) Equity.

It is argued that the preferred stock capacity of a company is distinct from its debt capacity because the legal obligation of paying interest on debt creates a risk of insolvency while the discretionary obligation of paying preferred dividend does not. Thus preferred stock may be used in addition to debt rather than as a substitute for it.

From the view point of the company the preference share financing offers following advantages:

(*i*) In contrast to bonds, it does not carry any fixed interest payment obligation.

(*ii*) A company with high rate of earnings may increase the owners' earnings by using securities carrying fixed return such as debentures or preference shares.

(*iii*) The finance manager by selling preferred stock instead of equity avoids the provision of equal participation in earnings.

(*iv*) In contrasts as to bonds it enables the firm to conserve mortgageable assets.

(*v*) It provides flexibility in capital structure.

Disadvantages

The preference shares must be sold at a higher yield basis than that of bonds (Even then the preference shares are not popular in the Indian market).

The preference dividend is not deductible as a tax expense which makes their cost differential very great in comparison to bonds. (This fact has greatly reduced the use of this source of finance).

Debt Financing: Loan Capital Debentures

Loan capital does not provide the lender with a share in the ownership of the company. Debentures are loans which are usually secured on all the assets of a company by a floating charge and will be for some fixed period of say fifteen or twenty years. The interest payable on the loan is a first priority for the company, whether it makes a profit or a loss, thus the payments are tax-deductible. However, in times of high inflation interest rates of straight loans have tended to be very high. As a result, most companies which issue debentures add an 'equity sweetener' to make the loan more palatable. This means that conditions are attached to the loan which allow it to be converted into share capital at some future date. There are several ways of doing this. Interest rates on this kind of loan are much closer to the dividend yield on the company's shares and for a growth company (one that is retaining a lot of its profits for reinvestment: an obvious source of capital for an existing company) this may be much lower than the general level of interest rates.

Debentures

A debenture is a long-term promissory note or bond that may or may not be secured by a pledge of any specific property. However, like other general creditors claims' it is secured by any property not otherwise pledged.

Features

1. Entitled to periodic payment of interest
2. Entitled to redemption of their money
3. No voting rights
4. Usually secured by mortgage
5. Right to use the company for unpaid dues
6. Right to sell the security
7. Apply for foreclosure or winding up.

From the point of view of the management:

(*a*) Cost of debt is definitely known and limited.

(*b*) Debentures holders do not participate in super profits.

(*c*) Expected yield is lower than equity.

(*d*) Don't have to lose control or share control with debenture holders.

(*e*) Interest payment is a deductible tax expenditure.

(*f*) Provides flexibility in capital structure as they are redeemable at the option of the company.

(*g*) Management can take advantage of trading on equity. (*Ref. Chapter 2: Long-term Finance and Capital Structure*).

Disadvantages

1. Debt carries a fixed charge. Hence greater risk of earnings fluctuate.
2. High leverage may bring down the value of equity.
3. Carry a fixed maturity date hence repayment is arranged.
4. During depression phase of trade cycle they may cause trouble.
5. Debenture provides stringent conditions.

Different investors have different risk return trade-off preferences.

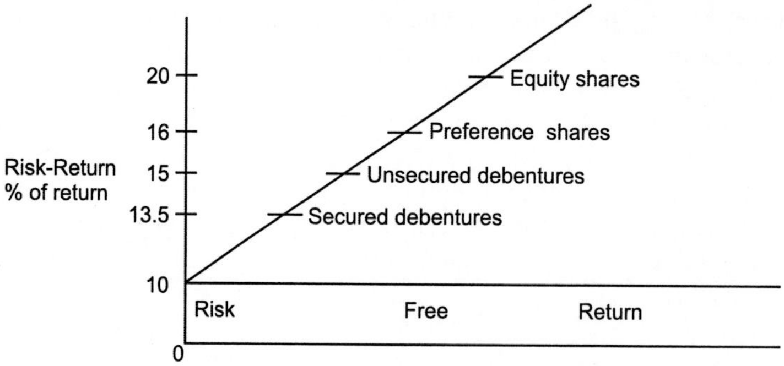

Fig. 2.1 Rationale for different types of securities

Long-term Debt

Debt may be used under following circumstances:

1. Sales and earnings are stable-relatively or rising.
2. Existing debt ratio is relatively low.
3. Control considerations are significant.
4. Restrictions and bond indenture are not serious.

Mortgage Debenture

Mortgage debentures are secured by a fixed charge on specific assets of the company, usually land and buildings. A large company will sell these in the form of stocks, in units of say ₹ 100 upwards. A smaller company will probably obtain its money from one lender. The mortgage market is not as strong as it was; inflation has a tendency to eat into investments of this sort and for this reason most institutions prefer sale and lease-back. The smaller the company the more difficult the mortgage. Since the Building Societies Regulations, building societies have been much restricted in the business field and insurance companies are the principal source for small mortgages.

Venture Capital

A venture capitalist is a person or an organization prepared to participate in a business. The venture capitalist thus becomes part owner, with a say in what the business does. The venture capitalists are usually involved in small to medium-sized businesses (large companies can obtain capital more easily). They are looking for a high rate of return, probably not less than 30 percent. Part of this return may be in the form of a capital gain, so they are also looking for good growth prospects plus the opportunity to resell their investment (to you or somebody else) in the future. To persuade a venture capital institution to invest in a company usually requires that you present an outstanding case.

Most businesses need medium-term funds, that is to say, borrowing from two to ten years, which commits them only for a limited period of time. Various sources of medium-term capital are available.

Sources of Medium-term Capital

Some sources of medium-term capital are:

1. *Government*:

   In development areas which may very well lend to development projects, government may make building grants up to say 35 per cent of construction or conversion costs, removal grants to cover relocation and low interest loans for working capital and plant. These may be accompanied by other tax concessions.

2. *Finance corporations*:

   There are two of these, the Industrial Finance Corporation (I.F.C.I.) for industries which is concerned with large projects, especially those of national importance, and the State Finance Corporation (S.F.C). The latter is more important in the medium-term field.

3. *Merchant banks*:

   The banks are usually interested in a firm at the stage where it has several years of profitable operation and can put substantial sums of money to immediate good use. These banks look for a quick turn round of funds to that, ideally, it is looking to invest for three to four years making maximum per cent on the deal; as well as taking a share of the equity. They invariably insist on representation on the board of directors. Not all merchant banks are restricted to venture capital operations and some will make fixed-term loans without equity involvement to suitable companies.

4. *Commercial banks*:

   All the commercial banks have merchant bank subsidiaries. Their activities now go further than the provision of venture capital of the merchant banking kind. They are prepared to consider fixed-term lending of even small amounts (say over one to seven years) which may be used for working capital or purchase of plant. The pattern of repayment is usually on a monthly basis combining principal and interest.

5. *Provident fund and pension funds*:

   Some provident and pension funds are prepared to provide medium-term finance of the venture capital type. Terms are similar to those of a merchant bank.

6. *Insurance companies*:

   These are not very active in the venture capital field, but it may occasionally be possible to obtain a medium-term mortgage from this source.

7. *Finance houses*:

   The larger finance houses provide medium-term lending facilities. They will usually favour existing customers such as a company that is already using them for say hire-purchase, and will require security for the loan such as a property mortgage.

8. *Miscellaneous*:

   A number of other institutions may be approached for small scale industries in the rural areas.

SHORT-TERM FINANCE

The financial strategy of a project must allow a degree of flexibility to respond to inevitable change in its environment. Short-term finance is an important aspect of this flexibility. Short-term financing is concerned with raising money which is needed for a short-period of time usually less than a year. Various sources of short-term credit include trade credit, bank credit, advance from customers, installment credit and accounts receivable financing.

Sources of Short-term Finance

1. ***Bank Overdrafts***:

   An overdraft is a facility, not a loan. It allows a company to draw cheques up to a pre-arranged limit. Interest is calculated on the overdraft on a day-to-day basis which makes it very flexible; on the other hand it is legally repayable on demand. However, it is a useful and cheap source of funds for emergencies and for temporary purposes, such as building up inventories before a busy season. The banks are not pawnbrokers, they are not been to get involved in the business of taking over and selling off assets. Applications for funds should therefore be supported by well documented and detailed cash flow forecasts which show how the overdraft will be serviced.

2. ***Suppliers finance***:

   The best example of this in the hospitality industry and the brewery companies which will lend money for improvement of premises or purchase of equipment. Formal credit arrangements may also be made for general purchases. Some hotels extend this beyond the agreed period as an apparently 'free' source of funds. The hidden costs of this practice in terms of poorer service and bad credit ratings can be substantial.

3. ***Customer finance***:

   In the hospitality business, in order to avoid carrying large debts such as those associated with banqueting, the hotel can set up a schedule of payments such as an advance deposit, a proportion to be paid with seven days of the event, balance in thirty days. There is also a good credit control, prompt rendering of invoices and fast collection procedures to avoid tying up capital unnecessarily. If the risks of non-payment are considered unacceptable then insurance may be purchased.

4. ***Bank Credit***:

   Commercial banks play a very important role in financing the short-term requirements of the business firms. They provide finance by way of loans, cash credit, overdrafts and discounting of bills. Banks grant credit on the security of goods, documents, shares and debentures, life insurance policies and fixed deposited.

5. ***Trade Credit***:

   A business house may grant credit to its customers who buy goods from it and in the same way it gets credit from its suppliers. Thus, trade credit is a credit extended by the sellers to the buyers at all levels of production and distribution. It does not need any security except the reputation of the firm. It does not bring cash but delay payment against purchases.

6. ***Instalment Credit***:

   A business house may buy equipment on instalment basis. Some amount is paid immediately on signing the agreement and rest is paid in 10 to 12 instalments spread over a year or two.

7. ***Customer Advance***:

   Many times, the manufacturers insist on advance from customers against their orders. This advance, sometimes, play a significant role in short–term financing. The Lohia Machines Ltd., Maruti Udyog and Bajaj Auto Ltd., have gathered huge amounts as advance from customers against their orders.

Illustration 2.1

M/s Adam Limited has a present annual sales turnover of ₹ 4,00,00,000. The unit sale price is ₹ 20. The variable cost are ₹ 12 per unit and fixed costs amount of ₹ 50,00,000 per annum. The present credit period of one month is proposed to be extended to either 2 or 3 months whichever will be more profitable. The following additional information is available:

	On the basis of Credit Period		
	1 month	**2 months**	**3 months**
Increase in sales by	–	10%	30%
% of bad debts to sales	1	2	5

Fixed cost will increase by ₹ 75,000 when sales will increase by 30%. The company requires a pre-tax return on investment at 20%.

Evaluate the profitability of the proposals and recommended best credit period for the company.

Solution:

Evaluation of Profitability under different credit periods

Particulars	One month	Two months	Three months
Sales	₹ 4,00,00,000	₹ 4,40,00,000	₹ 5,20,00,000
Bad debt to sales	4,00,000	8,80,000	26,00,000
Net sales	**3,96,00,000**	**4,31,20,000**	**4,94,00,000**
Net incremental sales (A)	–	35,20,000	98,00,000
Cost of sales:			
Variable cost @ ₹ 12	2,40,00,000	2,64,00,000	3,12,00,000
Fixed cost	50,00,000	50,00,000	57,50,000
Cost of sales	**2,90,00,000**	**3,14,00,000**	**3,69,50,000**
Net incremental cost (B)	–	24,00,000	79,50,000
Average debtors at cost	24,16,667	52,33,333	92,37,500
	(2,90,00,000 ÷ 12)	(3,14,00,000 ÷ 6)	(3,69,50,000 ÷ 4)
Cost of incremental debtors @ 20% (C)	–	56,3333	1,36,4170
Total incremental cost (B + C)	–	29,63,330	93,14,170
Net increase in profit [A – (B + C)]	–	**5,56,670**	**4,85,830**

The change of credit period from one month to two months is expected to increase the profit by ₹ 55,667 which is more than ₹ 48,583. So, the firm may change its credit policy from the present credit period of one month to two months.

Sale and Leaseback

This is a very popular method of financing in a business and has been used by many companies of all kinds. It is available to organizations which own, or hold on long lease properties in good condition. It does not increase the capital employed. Mortgages usually raise only between 40 and 75 per cent of the value of the property, which is still owned by the company. Sale and leaseback raises 100 per cent of the effective valuation and is a means of converting fixed capital into cash. Thus its relates to a separation of the investment in buildings and plant and operating equipment.

The method of operation is that the building (or even fixed plant) is sold to an insurance company or pension fund (or may be a unit trust) and is then leased back at an agreed percentage (which may increase over time). If a buy-back clause is included in the sale contract the method may be used as a continuing means of finance. For example, a company may sell its hotel for say ₹ 700 million with an option to repurchase it in ten years time for say ₹ 1,000 million. If it has done its sums right, the building may then be resold immediately for more than ₹ 1,000 million. The main advantage of the method is that it is available when all other methods are cut off and it allows the hotel to invest its main capital in the business it understands best the hotel business—where it can make the highest return; the property business if left to others.

This method has its drawbacks. It reduces the hotel's borrowing potential in other ways (there are no longer any big fixed assets to offer as colateral), the rent has to be found no matter what the circumstances, and the business loses the capital appreciation of the property. It works out very expensive in the long run. Rent reviews may take place as frequently as every five years and this can push the cost of the capital way over that which might be obtained via a mortgage.

Invoice Discounting and Sales Factoring

These techniques are not widely used by many companies. Invoice discounting involves the sale of customer debts for the sole purpose of releasing the capital locked up in them. It reduces the need for funds while not increasing the company's liabilities. The factor agrees to reimburse the business house at once for the face value of debts up to a given limit, at a certain interest charge of say one per cent per month. When the business house has collected the debt it pays the factor back. Thus the customers are not aware of the deal, unlike the situation with sales factoring, which transfers all responsibility for debt collection to the factor, who pays the business immediately for up to 80 per cent of the debt. Sales factoring removes the need for sales ledger accounting from the hotel and allows for accurate cash budgeting.

Equipment Leasing and Hire Purchase

These are two methods of financing a company which do not involve raising capital:

(*i*) Equipment leasing, and

(*ii*) Hire-purchase.

They are principally funded by finance houses and merchant banks, though other institutions may be involved. Almost anything can be financed in this way since it is not the nature of the goods that matter but the creditworthiness of the company.

Both leasing and H.P. are easy to arrange and the market is competitive. So contracts should be scrutinised to obtain the best deal. H.P. is usually arranged for a shorter period (up to three years) and involves payments of a deposit. On the other hand although cash outgoing may be heavier, it is usually much cheaper than leasing and leaves the company with ownership of the asset.

The choice of method revolves around cash flow. Tax relief's may be associated with the purchase of an asset or with leasing and H.P. payments. Regular future payments themselves have implications but these may be offset if the benefit derived from use of the asset (extra profit) is high or if inflation is running at a high level.

Franchising

Franchising is a contractual relationship between two parties which is of mutual benefit to their shared business activities. The first party of the contract is the *franchisor*. This may refer to an individual or company who has devised a successful format for operating. This may include methods of design and construction, established procedures and management methods. All based on an acceptable marketing posture.

The franchisor is prepared to let the second party to the contract, the *franchisee,* use his ideas in return for certain payments and guarantees. Thus the franchisee may have to raise the capital for the project but will be able to use the expertise to the franchisor in the design and operation. The franchisee will continue to receive support and advice from the franchisor after the property is open. The payment or licence fee for these services may take several forms. In the case of a hotel it might be in the nature of a one-off fee for the initial advice and then a continued fee for marketing and management service.

The advantages to both parties are considerable. Since each franchisee is bringing in his or her own capital, the franchisor can expand much more rapidly than if he was dependent on his own resources. He has reduced his own capital involvement (risk) and at the same time provided a continuing inflow of funds.

For the franchisee, the operator, capital is often easier to raise for a tried and tested business system than for one that is completely new, the risk of failure is reduced by the expertise and help of the franchisor and he can accrue some of the benefits of a large company, brand image, marketing operation within the framework of his own business.

Both parties have a vested interest in success. The franchisor wants to attract other franchisees and to guarantee his cash inflow and the franchisee has the motivation of his own business with his own capital at risk.

The cornerstone of most franchises is a standardized product. This is where most of the big company benefits, and particularly the marketing benefits, pay off. This is the heart of the franchise and also its weakest point, because this is where all the problems lie. As the franchisee becomes more experienced and confident there is a tendency to want to 'improve' or change things, both to improve profitability and to personalize the business. Such change undermine the standardization of the product, and in effect, weaken the marketing base of the whole chain leading to problems of control.

Management Contracts

A management contract is an agreement between the owner of a building and the operator. The owner agrees to provide the capital and to sustain all or some of the loss in return for a share of the profits (if any). The operator agrees to assume all responsibility for the day-to-day operation of the property, may provide some of the operating equipment and usually agrees to use his brand name or trade mark. As a method of operation it involves very little risk for the operator and yet allows extension of geographic market coverage. It was devised for situations in which the major international chains were asked to open property in parts of the world of uncertain political and economic stability. The deal is not quite so one-sided as it may appear. The operator has to maintain a certain standard in order to protect his corporate image and in countries with little hotel expertise. It is a good way of benefiting from some of the best management systems around (plus associated training for local staff) and linking with an established marking network.

Growth in the adoption of management contracts has been spectacular. The increase in the growth of management contracts has been due to a combination of factors. A government building incentive scheme coupled with a boom attracted many inexperienced companies into the business in the early 1970s which soon ran into trouble. More recently the poor economic climate, crippling taxation system and high cost of land have meant that management contracts have represented one means of expansion.

The key to a management contract lies in its fee structure. This fee structure is illustrated in Table 2.1.

Table 2.1 Different fee structures in a management contract

1.	Suppose revenue	₹ 250,000,000		
2.	G.O.P	₹ 200,000,000		
3.	Net profit	₹ 50,000,000		
	% of fee structures			
		A	B	C
	Share of gross revenue	3%	—	3%
	Share of gross operating profit	12.5%	25%	—
	Share of net income	—	—	50%
	Total fees payable	**₹ 2,00,000**	**25,00,000**	**32,50,000**

Details of each individual contracts may vary enormously and range from payments of fixed amounts to complicated percentage systems levied on different levels and sources of profit. The contract must refer to the timing of payments. It must define all terms and treatment of charges carefully, otherwise it might be possible for the business make a book loss under any circumstances. There is also a provision which allows for inspections of accounts. On the operators side, the main area of concern is to regulate charge levied on gross revenue. This yields a high income for the landlord but also shifts the breakeven point of the whole operation which may make it difficult to make profits.

CAPITAL STRUCTURE DECISION

The word 'capital' has a very wide variety of meanings. The economists speak of 'capital' as that part of wealth which is used for further production. Businessmen view the word 'capital' in the sense of total assets employed (total funds employed) in the business. The accountant uses the term 'capital' to mean the net assets or the net-worth as given in the balance sheet. In legal terms it refers to the funds raised through equity shares only. As the different securities, *viz.*, the equity shares, preference shares, and debentures have not only different costs involved but also these have different characteristics in terms of flexibility, redeem ability and availability for different periods of time, the management is confronted with the problem of deciding a ratio in which different sources of capital be used to raise, the total funds needed to carry on business. This is precisely the subject matter of capital structure.

In simple terms the capital structure may be defined as the make up of capitalisation. While capitalisation refers to the total amount of funds needed to run a business. In other words the capital structure decision is concerned with the determination of the ratio which different types of securities will bear to total capitalisation. A company's capital structure is said to be high-geared when it has used borrowings much more than equity in its total capital. It would be low geared when proportion of debt is low as compared to equity. For example, if a company has raised ₹ 25,00,000 by way of debentures and ₹ 10,00,000 by way of equity shares, it is said to be high levered or high goal capital structure. Thus, in capital structure decision the manager is concerned with the following issues:

1. How much will be the equity money?
2. How much will be borrowed?
3. What should be debt-equity mix so as to maximize the value of the firm?

A student of finance knows that the interest on loan/debentures because of its tax-deductible nature, under favourable economic conditions, enhances or increase the earning per share available to equity owners. But the use of debt increase the financial risks of the shareholders. As a result it can not be stated definitely whether or not the value of the firm (as judged by the market price of its shares) will increase with leverage.

DETERMINANTS OF CAPITAL STRUCTURE

If leverage affects the cost of capital and the value of the firm, an optimum capital structure will be obtained at such a judicious mix of equity and debt where the cost of capital is minimum and the value of the firm maximum. The question of the existence of optimum capital structure has been put by Ezra Solomon, "Given that a firm has a particular structure of assets which gives net operating income of a given size and quality and given a structure of rates in the capital market, is there some specific degree of financial leverage at which the market value of the firm's securities will be higher than at other degrees of leverages?"

If it is so, there is an optimal capital structure. However, in theory it is possible to define an optimum capital structure but in practice it is rather very difficult to discover the level of debt and equity that maximize the value of the firm.

The factors that determine the capital structure are as given in Fig. 2.2

Determinants of Capital Structure

Internal Factors

1. Trading on equity
2. Nature of business
3. Desire to retain control
4. Purpose of financing
5. Period for which funds are needed
6. Existing capital structure
7. Expected rate of growth
8. Philosophy of management.

External Factors

1. Statement of the market
2. Requirements of investors
3. Cost of raising funds
4. Legal requirement
5. Level of interest rates
6. Availability of funds.
7. Tax policy on interest and dividend.

Fig. 2.2 Determinants of capital structure.

Internal Factors

1. Trading on Equity or Financial Leverage

When a company uses both debt and equity capital in the regular conduct of its business, it is said to be trading on equity. While taking a decision regarding the capital structure, the financial manager must look into the benefit that the use of debt brings to the equity owners.

For example, suppose 'A' and 'B' are two corporate houses in the same industry. These two house are identical in all respects excepts that of their capital structure.

Comparative Capital Structure

Particulars	Company A	Company B
Total Funds employed	**₹ 20,00,000**	**20,00,000**
Raised from equity (₹ 10 each)	₹ 20,00,000	10,00,000
15% debenture	–	10,00,000
Both company A and B earn 25% on funds employed		
Hence EBIT (Earnings before Interest and taxes)	5,00,000	5,00,000
Less interest on debentures	–	1,50 000
Taxable Income	5,00,000	3,50,000
Suppose tax rate is 50%	2,50,000	1,75,000
Profit after tax	2,50,000	1,75,000
On 2,00,000 shares EPS (Earning per share)	**1.25**	
On 1,00,000 share EPS		**1.75**

Thus it is evident from the foregoing that the earnings available to equity get magnified due to the use of debt which carries less risk and is comparatively cheaper/economical for the company. This concept is called trading in equity because debentures holders buy debentures looking to equity which is their safety margin. In the event, of closure, the debenture holders will get their contribution back much earlier than equity. For example if in case of company B the loss is say ₹ 10,00,000 the debenture holders would still get their full refund while equity holders may get nothing. Trading on equity is favourable so long as the rate of earnings (in our example 25%), exceeds the committed rate of interest (in our case 15%). Before taking advantage through trading on equity, the management must ensure that the business operations are non-speculative and there is stability of earnings.

2. Nature of Business

Another factor that must be taken care of while deciding about capital structure is the nature of business or enterprises, *i.e.*, whether it is manufacturing, merchandising, financing, extraction or public utility type. Public utilities due to their stable earnings and having little competion can easily raise funds from interest bearing securities like bonds. Manufacturing-cum-marketing organization must depend more on equity.

3. Desire to Retain Control

When retention of control is of paramount importance funds must be raised only by debt or by preference shares because these do not enjoy voting rights.

4. Purpose of Financing

The funds may be needed either for a productive or for a non-productive purpose. In the later case there is no increase in income. As such it is advisable for the management to have incremental income.

5. Period for Which Funds are Needed

As a general rule debt should be used for short period requirements so that the same can be returned as and when the company generates its own funds. Thus for periods upto 5 to 7 years, debentures may be used as in case of equity shares, the money once raised cannot be returned even if not needed after some time.

6. Existing Capital Structure

Before one takes a decision about the mix of debt and equity, it is imperative to look at the existing capital gearing, *i.e.*, the extent to which funds from borrowings have already been raised. In case debt has not been used at all, it makes a good case for debt utilisation.

7. Expected Rate of Growth

When the company expects a high rate of growth, which means more inflows coupled with more requirements of funds, it would be appropriate to strike balance between debt and equity. However, debt upto a particular level can be safely used in this case.

8. Management's Attitude Towards Risks

It is a known fact that raising of funds through debt increases the financial risk involve, *i.e.*, as the debt implies a fixed interest burden on the company, the non-payment of which can cause technical insolvency. Thus, if the management is risk taking management, more debt may be resorted to while equity may be used if the philosophy is to avoid risk-taking.

In addition to the above, companies having an asset structure comprising more of fixed assets when current assets can affort to use debt in combination with equity as these fixed assets provide a safety margin for these debt securities.

Further, use of debt on preference shares lends more flexibility to its capital structure. The management must bear in mind that the capital structure should not be very complex. However, internally the management must look to certainty, adequacy and regularity of earnings (cash in flows) before deciding the make up its capitalisation.

External Factors

1. Sentiment of the Market

Management's decision alone can hardly be of any use if it is not in line with the mood of the investor as these securities are to be purchased by them. There are periods when people like equity or debentures. If they want safety of funds, debentures may get preference over equity. Thus the mood of the market must be carefully analysed before deciding about the source of funds.

2. Requirement of Investors

Different investors, for various reasons, have different requirement. For example retired people in an advanced age may require safety of funds as well as regularity and certainty of returns from their investment. In such a situation debentures may be ideal security. There are others who want to take risk and hope to get higher returns and capital appreciation in which case equity may meet their requirements.

3. Cost of Raising Funds

It is also to be considered before taking a capital structure decision. Normally, equity issue is a lightly costlier than debt. Retained earnings may prove to be more economical. However, this factor plays only a limited role in modern days.

4. Legal Requirements

Capital structure planning also needs complying with legal rules and provisions. For example banking companies in India can raise money only by the issue of equity and not by bonds. Similarly, under 'Acceptance to Public Deposit' Rules 1974' a company can not raise more than 15 per cent of its paid up capital plus reserves by way of public deposits.

5. Tax Rates

As is well known, interest is now-a-days, paid on debt prior to calculation of corporate income tax, while preference dividend and equity dividend is paid after tax calculations. This factor has severely affected the use of preference shares as a security. Companies in high tax brackets tend to use preference shares as a security. Companies in high tax brackets tend to use more debt than otherwise.

Illustration 2.2

Exaplain the Modigliani–Miller theory on the effect of gearing on the cost of capital to, and value of the firm, in the absence of taxation. Explain how the theory is adjusted to take into account the effects of taxation. What arc thc principal weaknesses of this theory?

Solution:

The MM theory of capital structure differs from the traditional view in its assumptions about shareholders behaviour. The MM theory negates the view that there can be an optimum level of gearing which can reduce the cost of capital and maximize the value of the firm. Modiliani and Miller proved that the value of the firm is dependent upon the income generated from the business activities of a firm and not the way in which this income is allocated between the providers of capital. If the shares of two firms with different level of gearing but the same level of business risk are traded at different prices, then shareholders will switch their investment from the overvalued to the undervalued firm. Simultaneously they will adjust their level of personal borrowing through the market in order to maintain their overall level of business risk at the same level. This process, which is known as arbitrage will result in the firms having the same equilibrium total value.

When taxation is introduced into the model, the total market value of the firm is not independent of its capital structure. This is because of the tax shield provided by loans, the interest on which is treated as a charge in the financial statements. The market value of the firm, in such a situation increases with gearing, the amount of increase being the present value of the tax shield on the interest payments. This also implies that the WACC declines as gearing increases.

The main weaknesses of the theory are as follows:

1. In defining the arbitrage process it is assumed that personal borrowing is a perfect substitute for corporate borrowing. This is unlikely to be true in actual practice.
2. It is assumed that all earnings are paid out as dividends.
3. It is difficult to identify firms with the same business risk.
4. It is difficult to identify two firms with the same operating profile.

Illustration 2.3

Three companies J, G and R are in the same type of business and hence have similar operating risks. However, the capital structure of each of them is different and the following are the details:

Capital Structure of J, G and R

Particulars	J	G	R
Equity share capital	₹ 4,00,000	₹ 2,50,000	₹ 5,00,000
[Face value ₹ 10 per share]			
Market value per share	15	20	12
Dividend per share	2.70	4	2.88
Debentures	–	1,00,000	2,50,000
[Face value per debenture ₹ 100]			
Market value per debenture	–	125	80
Interest rate	–	10%	8%

You are required to calculate WACC of J, G and R.

Solution:

Calculation of WACC of J, G and R

Particulars	Amount	Weights	After tax cost	Weighted cost
(*i*) Cost of capital of shares at market value				
J	₹ 6,00,000	1.00	(2.70/15) = 18%	18%
G	5,00,000	0.80	(4.20) = 20%	16%
R	6,00,000	0.75	(2.88/12) = 24%	18%
(*ii*) Cost of capital of debenture at market value				
J	–	–	–	–
G	₹ 1,25,000	0.20	(10/125) (1 – 0.5) = 4%	0.80%
R	2,00,000	0.25	(8/80) (1 – 0.5) = 5%	1.25%

Weighted average cost of capital

J	18% + 00% = 18%
G	16% + 0.8% = 16.8%
R	18% + 1.25% = 19.25%.

Illustration 2.4

M/s L & T limited provides you with the following figures:

	₹
Profit	3,00,000
Less: Interest on debentures @ 12%	60,000
	2,40,000
Income-tax @ 50%	1,20,000
	1,20,000
Number of equity shares (₹ 10 each)	40,000
E.P.S. (Earning per share)	₹ 3
Ruling price in market	₹ 30
PE ratio (Market price/EPS)	10

The company has undistributed reserves of ₹ 6,00,000. The company needs ₹ 2,00,000 for expansion. This amount will earn at the same rate as funds already employed. You are informed that a debt equity ratio $\left(\frac{\text{Debt}}{\text{Debt + Equity}}\right)$ higher than 35% will push the P/E ratio down to 8 and raise the interest rate on additional amount borrowed to 14%.

You are required to ascertain the probable price of the share:

(*i*) If the additional funds are raised as debt; and

(*ii*) If the amount is raised by issuing equity shares.

Solution:

Calculation of probable price of shares of M/s L & T Limited

Particulars	Amount	
	Case (*i*) If ₹ 2,00,000 is borrowed	Case (*ii*) If ₹ 2,00,000 is raised by issue of equity shares
	₹	₹
Earnings before interest and tax (EBIT): 20% on ₹ 17,00,000	3,40,000	3,40,000
[Refer to working note (*i*)]		
Less: Debenture interest:		
Old 12% on ₹ 5,00,000	60,000	60,000
New 14% on ₹ 2,00,000	28,000	-
Earnings before tax (EBT)	**2,52,000**	**2,80,000**
Income-tax @ 50%	1,26,000	1,40,000
Profit after tax	**1,26,000**	**1,40,000**
Total number of shares	40,000	46,667
Earnings per share (EPS)	3.15	3
P/E ratio	8	10
Market price per share	**15.20**	**30**

It has been assumed that the additional amount will be raised by issuing 6,667 shares @ ₹ 30 per share. However, in practice, the issue price will be substantially lower than ₹ 30.

Working notes:

(*i*) Capital employed at present:

	₹
Debentures $\left(₹\,60{,}000 \times \frac{100}{12}\right)$	5,00,000
Share capital	4,00,000
Reserves	6,00,000
Total	15,00,000

(*ii*) Rate of return at present: $\frac{₹\,3{,}00{,}000}{₹\,15{,}00{,}000} \times 100 = 20\%$

(*iii*) Debt/Equity ratio if ₹ 2,00,000 is borrowed $= \frac{₹\,7{,}00{,}000}{₹\,17{,}00{,}000} \times 100 = 41.2\%$

Therefore, P/E ratio in such a case would be ₹ 8.

Illustration 2.5

M/s Duccan Ltd. is now extending 1 month's credit to its selected customers. It sells its product at ₹ 100 each, and has an annual sales volume of 60,000 units. At current level of production, which matches with sales, the product has a total cost of ₹ 90 per unit and a variable cost of ₹ 80 per unit. The company is considering a plan to grant more liberal terms by extending the duration of credit from 1 month to 2 months and expects the sales to the customer group to go up by 25 per cent. In the background of a normal expectation of a 20 per cent return on investment, will this relaxation in credit standard justify itself.

Solution:

(*i*) Calculation of profit on additional sales

Particulars	Detail	Amount
Selling price per unit	₹ 100	
Less: Variable cost per unit	80	
Marginal contribution/unit	20	
Number of additional units to be sold	20 × 15,000	₹ 3,00,000

(*ii*) Cost of additional investment in receivables

(*a*) Average investments in receivables:
Present plan = (60,000 units × ₹ 90)/Debtors turnover, 12(12 ÷ 1) = ₹ 4,50,000
Proposed plan: [(60,000 units × ₹ 90) + (15,000 units × ₹ 80)/6 (12 ÷ 1)] = ₹ 11,00,000

(*b*) Additional investments in receivables = ₹ 11,00,000 – ₹ 4,50,000 = ₹ 6,50,000

(*c*) Cost of additional investments in receivables = 0.20 × ₹ 6,50,000 = ₹ 1,30,000

(*iii*) Summary

Profits on additional sales	₹ 3,00,000
Less: Increased cost of investments	1,30,000
Net increase in profits	1,70,000

Thus, the relaxation of credit standards is justified.

Illustration 2.6

M/s Medanta City Ltd. is presently financed entirely by equity shares. The current market value is ₹ 6,00,000. A dividend of ₹ 1,20,000 has just been paid. This level of dividend is expected to be paid indefinitely. The company is thinking of investing in a new project involving an outlay of ₹ 5,00,000 now and is expected to generate net cash receipts of ₹ 1,05,000 per annum indefinitely. The project would be financed by issuing ₹ 5,00,000 debentures at the market interest rate of 18%. Ignoring tax consideration:

You are required to:

(*i*) Calculate the value of equity shares and the gain made by the shareholders if the cost of equity rises to 21.6%.

(*ii*) Prove that the weighted average cost of capital is not affected by gearing.

Solution:

M/s Medanta City Ltd.

(*i*) Calculation of value of Equity share and the gains made by shareholders

	₹	
Project Cash inflows	1,05,000	
Less: Debenture interest [18% × 5,00,000]	90,000	
Surplus available for dividends	15,000	
Original dividend	1,20,000	
Increased dividend	1,35,000	
Value of equity (Dividend ÷ C/C)	$\frac{1,35,000}{0.216}$	= 6,25,000
Original value		6,00,000
Gains to shareholders		**25,000**

(*ii*) Calculation of new WACC

	MV (₹)	Proportion	Cost	WACC
Shares	6,25,000	5/9	21.6%	12%
Debentures	5,00,000	4/9	18.0%	8%
				20%

Existing WACC: As there is no debt capital at present, the cost of capital of equity will be its WACC also.

Therefore, $k_e = \frac{\text{Dividends}}{\text{Market value of equity}} = \frac{1,20,000}{6,00,000} \times 100 = 20\%$

Hence, there is no effect on WACC if the firm raises ₹ 5,00,000 debenture at the rate of 18%.

REVIEW QUESTIONS

1. (*a*) Compare debt and equity as sources of long-term funds.
   (*b*) Do you recommend the use of both in a company's capital structure? It so, why?
2. Define the term capital structure.
3. Explain briefly the determinants of capital structure decision.

Chapter 3

Analysis of Financial Statements

The best use of financial statements is their proper analysis, understanding the contents and use in the decision making process for the managements. Analysis of financial statements may be broadly categorized as under:

1. Financial Statements–their nature, and limitations
2. Meaning of Analysis of financial statements
3. Tools
4. Ratio Analysis
5. Funds Flow Analysis
6. Cash Flow Analysis.

A financial statement is a collection of data organized according to logical and consistent accounting, concepts, conventions and procedures. It is prepared with a view to understand certain financial aspects of a firm. As there are various parties having varied interests in an enterprise (equity shareholders, debenture holders, long-term loan suppliers, IDBI, IFCI, ICICI etc., and short-term creditors), these financial statements are used to inform these people about the financial position. Thus, the financial statements present a periodical review or report on the economical and financial activities of a company during a particular period of time. Unlike a sole proprietorship or partnership where preparation of the annual (or half yearly) accounts, viz, Trading and Profit and Loss Account and the Balance Sheet is desirable but not compulsory, a limited company is compulsorily required to prepare its financial statements. Section 210 of the Indian Companies Act, deals with the preparation of such financial statement. In case of a limited company these financial statements include a Trading and Profit and Loss Account (or simply and Income Statement) which should give a true and fair view of the profit and loss of the company for the financial year and a Balance Sheet which must show a true and fair view of the state of affairs of the business on a particular date. Financial statements, in case of companies also include a profit and loss appropriation A/C which shows the disbursement or allocation of profits among different heads. Besides these three statements, some companies voluntarily prepare and submit a Funds Flow Statement to its equity owners.

A proper analysis of these statements needs an understanding of these statements and various terms used therein.

BALANCE SHEET

A balance sheet is a financial statement which shows the financial position of a company or a firm as on a specific date usually at the close of the last day in a month or accounting period. It is a statement and not an account. The right hand side of the balance sheet shows resources, *i.e.,* assets and the left hand side shows how these resources are provided by equity and debt-liabilities. Thus a balance sheet provides a snapshot of the firm's financial position at the end of a period. As the name implies the totals of both sides–the assets and liabilities must be equal (balance).

Balance Sheet is a Measure of Financial Health of the Organization

In a balance sheet there appear all account which have balances. Various accounts such purchases, sales, rent, wages, stock, salaries, etc. have no balance as these are closed at the end of a period by transferring to the Trading and Profit and Loss Account to arrive at a result profit or loss. But there are other accounts such as Furniture, Buildings, Debtors, Creditors and Capital accounts etc. which are not closed down and are carried forward to next year. These have balances and therefore appear in the balance sheet, through which one can measure the financial health of a company.

Balance Sheet is a Statement of Assets and Liabilities

As stated earlier a balance sheet when prepared in a **'T'** shaped statement shows on the left hand side all accounts having credit balances technically called 'liabilities' and on the right hand side, it shows all accounts with debit balances known as 'assests'.

Balance sheet is a statements showing sources and uses of capital. A balance sheet may also be viewed as a statement showing the various sources of capital (liabilities) and how these funds have been applied (assets).

Uses of a Balance Sheet

Balance Sheet reflects a firm's financial status on a particular date. It shows the cost (not the market value) of assets and how these have been financed *i.e.,* whether by equity or debts or by both.

The balance sheet provides valuable information to gain insight into the company's financial status. It allows a comparative evaluation of performance when data for more than on year is presented in its.

INCOME STATEMENT

An income statement is a report of firm's activities during a particular periods normally one year. It is known by different names such as Profit and Loss Account, Income Statement or a Statement of Earnings and Expenses. When prepared in traditional 'T' shaped way it shows on the right hand side all revenues, income or gains and on the debit side all expenses, and losses, etc. the net result of which is either profit or loss. Thus, the Profit and Loss Account gives information about:

(*a*) The revenues or incomes earned and other gains made by the concern, and

(*b*) Amount spent to earn the revenues, incomes or gains and other losses that may have been suffered.

(*c*) A Profit and Loss Account shows the results of a company's operations. The differences between (*a*) and (*b*) would be either profit or loss. *i.e.,* if (*a*) is bigger there is profit and there is a loss if (*b*) is bigger.

(*d*) In case of a limited company the profit and loss account is legally required to give a true and fair view of the profit earned or loss suffered during the year.

LIMITATIONS OF FINANCIAL STATEMENTS

Although the financial statements provide very useful information yet these suffer from various limitations.

1. Non-incorporation of all assets

A balance sheet is said to be a statement of all assets and liabilities, however, it fails to record and show one of its most important tangible source, viz., human resource which makes the future of an organization. Although efforts are being made to incorporate the value of human resources yet till date no agreement has reached with regard to the technique to incorporate human resource.

2. Over-looking the effect of inflation

Following the cost concept all assets in the balance sheet are shown at their acquisition cost less deprecation. The replacement value of these assets or their market value may by much different than the ones shown in the balance sheet. But this fact is not revealed in the balance sheet.

3. Observance of certain accounting concepts

The balance sheet and income statement is prepared based on certain concepts. For example based on 'going concern concept' assets are valued at their cost less depreciation whereas their real value may be much less than the book value or may be very much on the higher side.

4. Reflection of past and not future

An investor may be more interested to judge a company's position in future but the balance sheet and the income statement only tell about the past. Thus these are not very useful in indicating future health of the company.

5. Personal judgment and discretionary powers

The figures in the financial statements are determined by personal judgment. Provision of depreciation, valuation of inventory, and provision for bad and doubtful debts are likely to change the amount of profits and assets and liabilities and all these are subjects to personal judgment of the management.

6. Managerial manipulations

All financial statements are subject to managerial manipulations which fact remains concealed in the balance sheet or income statement. There are instances when bankers granted loans on the strength of a balance sheet and suffered a loss due to company's failure in the very next year. Post-martem analysis revealed the manipulation in stock valuation by the company, which the loan-sanctioning bankers could not judge.

7. Interim reports

The financial statements are only interim reports. True profit or loss can be ascertained only when the entire life is run over.

From the foregoing it is clear that the financial statements suffer from serious limitations due to which there is a need to analysis and interpret the financial data presented therein.

The analysis of financial statements means such a treatment of the figures contained in the financial statements, as would enable the analyst to diagnose (to judge) the financial health to the company. The financial health of the company refers to the liquidity and profitability *i.e.,* if a company has enough of liquidity (both short-term and long-term) and is capable of earning a reasonable rate of return on its investment, it is said to be financially sound.

Liquidity, in this context, refers to the ability of a company to discharge its maturing obligations. Thus, if a company is able to pay off its short-term and long-term liabilities (interest on loan and/or its creditors) on time, it is said to have liquidity. Non-meeting of these obligations can force the company to face technical insolvency. (This is insolvency caused by absence of liquid resources – cash to pay its maturing obligations even if the company may have fixed assets of billions of rupees). The term profitability means earnings fair rate of return on its investment.

To sum up, financial statement analysis is largely a study or relationships among the various factors in business as disclosed by a single set of statements and a study of the trend of these factors as shown in a series of statements.

The process of analyzing the financial statements requires re-arranging, comparing and evaluating the significance of figures given in these statements.

Interpretation which follows financial analysis is an attempt to reach a logical conclusion regarding the position of a company. However, analyzing and interpretation are considered as complimentary to each other.

TECHNIQUES OF FINANCIAL ANALYSIS

Based on the objective and the specialists conducting the analysis, there may be use of either internal or external analysis.

1. Internal analysis:

This is carried out by those who have an access to the books of accounts and all other information relating to financial performance. Invariably it is the management that conduct the internal type of analysis.

2. External analysis:

This is carried out by people external to the organizations. The analysis in this case, is entirely on the basis of published financial statements, namely the income statements and the balance sheet.

TOOLS OF FINANCIAL ANALYSIS

1. Comparative statements
2. Common size statements
3. Trend ratios
4. Ratio analysis
5. Funds flow and cash flow analysis.

1. Comparative Statements

Absolute money values of various items of financial statements are designed so as to show the increase or decrease in their values over a period of time. Such statements are necessary to study the trends and directions of movements in the financial position and operating results.

2. Common Size Statements

It case of comparative statements it is difficult to comprehend the changes over the years in relation to total assets, total liabilities and total capital. Similarly comparison of two firms in an industry is rather impossible through comparative statements. Thus, if items are presented as percentage or ratios of a total item, a common base for comparison is provided and analysis is possible. Each percentage shows the relation of the individual item to the total.

Illustration 3.1

From the following income statements and balance sheet prepare a Comparative Statement.

M/s ABC Ltd New Delhi
Income Statement

(₹ in 000)

Particular	Previous year (31.12.201?)	Current year (31.12.201?)	Particular	Previous year (31.12.201?)	Current year (31.12.201?)
To Cost of good sold	3,000	3,750	By Sales	4,000	5,000
To Operating expenses:					
- Administration	100	100			
- Selling	150	200			
To, Net profit	750	950			
	4,000	**5,000**		**4,000**	**5,000**

M/s ABC Ltd.
Balance Sheet
as on 31.12.201?(Previous year) and 31.12.201? (Current Year)

(₹ in 000)

Liabilities	Previous year	Current year	Assets	Previous year	Current year
Equity Share Capital	2,000	2,000	Land	500	500
6% Preference Share Capital	1,500	1,500	Building	1,500	1,350
6% Debentures	500	750	Plant	1,500	1,350
Reserves	1,000	1,225	Furniture	500	700
Current Liabilities			**Current Assents**		
Bills Payable	250	375	Cash	500	700
Accounts Payable	750	1,000	Accounts Receivable	1,000	1,500
Tax Payable	500	750	Stock	1,000	1,500
	6,500	**7,600**		**6,500**	**7,600**

Solution:

M/s ABC Ltd

Comparative Income Statement

For the year ending 31.12.201?... Previous year and 31.12.201?.... Current year

(₹ in '000)

Particular	Previous year	Current year	Increase decrease	Percentage
Sales	4,000	5,000	1,000	+25
Cost of Goods Sold	3,000	3,750	750	+25
	1,000	1,250	250	
Less Operating Expenses				
(*i*) Administrative	100	100	—	—
(*ii*) Selling	150	200	50	33.33
Total	250	300	50	20
Operating profit	750	950	200	26.67

M/s ABC Ltd

Comparative Balance Sheets

As on 31.12.201?... and 31/201?....

(₹ in 000)

Assets	Pervious year	Current year	Increase/Decrease	Percentage
Cash	500	700	200	+40
Accounts Receivables	1,000	1,500	500	+50
Stock	1,000	1,500	500	+50
	2,500	3,700	1,200	+48
Fixed Assets				
Land	500	500	—	—
Building	1,500	1,350	-150	-10
Plant	1,500	1,350	-150	-10
Furniture	500	700	+200	+40
	4,000	3,900	-100	-2.5
Total Assets	**6,500**	**7,600**	**+1100**	**+16.92**
Liabilities and Capital				
Bills payable	250	375	+125	+50
Accounts payable	750	1,000	+250	+33.33
Tax payable	500	750	+250	+50
	1,500	**2125**	**+625**	**+41.66**
Long-term Liabilities				
6% Debentures	500	750	250	+50
Total liabilities	**2,000**	**2,875**	**+875**	**43.75**

Capital and Reserves				
Equity capital	2,000	2,000	–	–
Reserves	1,000	1,225	225	22.5
Preference capital	1,500	1,500	–	–
Total Share holder's Funds	4,500	4,725	225	5
Total Liabilities and capital	**6,500**	**7,600**	**1,100**	**16.92**

Illustration 3.2

Based on the same set of figures as given in **Illustration 3.1,** prepare a common size income statements and balance sheets.

Solution:

M/s ABC Ltd., New Delhi
Common-size Income Statements
for Previous and Current year

Particulars	Pervious year	Current year
Sales	100	100
Cost of good sold	75	75
Gross profit	25	25
Operating expenses:		
Administration:		
Previous year $\left(\frac{100}{4,000}\times 100\right)$	2.5	
Current year $\left(\frac{100}{5,000}\times 100\right)$		2
Selling expenses	3.75	4
Total operating expenses	6.25	6
Operating profit	**18.75**	**19**

From the above it is evident that cost of goods sold remained constant even though it increased in absolute terms. Consequently, the gross profit ratio remains constant at 25%, on the same lines. It is clear that administrative expenses have gone down as a percentage of sales. But selling expenses have increased over this period. On the whole the operating profit has slightly gone up from 18.75 percent to 19 per cent.

M/s ABC Ltd. New Delhi
Common-size Balance Sheets

Particular	% Previous year	% Current year
Currents Assets		
Cash:		
Previous year = $\left(\frac{500}{6,500}\times\frac{100}{1}\right)$	7.70	
Current year = $\left(\frac{700}{7,600}\times\frac{100}{1}\right)$		9.21

Debtors or Accounts Receivable	15.38	19.74
Stock	15.38	19.74
	38.46	**48.69**
FIXED Assets		
Building	23.08	17.76
Plant	23.08	17.76
Furniture	7.70	9.21
Land	7.70	6.58
Total Fixed Assets	**61.54**	**51.31**
Total Assets	100	100
Liabilities Capital		
Current Liabilities:		
Bills payable	3.85	4.93
Accounts payable	11.54	13.16
Taxes payable	7.70	9.86
Total Current Liabilities	**23.07**	**27.95**
Long-term Liabilities:		
6% Debentures	7.69	9.87
Capital and Reserves:		
Equity capital	30.77	26.32
Reserves	15.9	16.12
Preference shares	23.08	19.74
Total Shareholder's Funds	69.24	62.17
Total Liabilities	76.93	72.04
Total Liabilities and Capital	**100**	**100**

Form the above it is clear that percentage of current assets has gone up from 38.46 in previous year to 48.69 in current year. Similarly, the percentage of current liabilities to total liabilities has gone up from 23.07 to 27.95 in current year. However, as the increase in current assets is higher than that of current liabilities the working capital (current assets minus current liabilities) has gone up. The percentage of shareholders funds has gone down from 69.24 in previous year to 62.17 in current year.

3. Trend Ratios

Trend percentages are of great help to indicate the pattern of movement of various figures. In this case a base year is decided and percentages are worked out for subsequent years. Such percentages may be calculated for major items in the financial statements.

4. Ratio Analysis

Capital employed in a corporate body can be determined by analysing either the liability side of the balance sheet, *i.e.*, net worth plus debt capital, or the asset side, *i.e.*, net fixed assets plus net current assets. Both will give the same result.

Operating profit is profit before depreciation, interest and tax. Though post-tax profit is returns available to owners, operating profit is considered here. Rate of interest, depreciation and tax liability differ for different companies, and vary annually for the same company.

To improve ROCE, a company has to improve:

(*a*) Turnover of capital employed or the ratio of sales to capital employed by maximizing sales on the one hand and minimizing capital employed one the other.

(*b*) Contribution to sale, which can be improved by exercising proper control on variable cost. Any improvement in this ratio helps in bringing down the break-even point for the company.

(*c*) Operate for above the break-even point or maintain higher margin of safety which is given as the ratio of operating profit to contribution.

The product of these three ratios is ROCE—the numerator of one ratio becoming the denominator of the other ratio.

An absolute figure often fails to communicate anything significant. Thus the information that company 'A' has made a profit of ₹ 10,00,000 carries no meaning unless we know the amount of capital employed or profit earned in the earlier year or years.

Ratio, *simply stated, is a mathematical expression of the relation existing between two or more figures. Accounting ratios are, therefore, relationship expressed in arithmetical terms between figures from financial statements.*

HOW TO EXPRESS A RATIO

Ratios are expressed in a number of ways. Pure ratios are arrived at by simple division of one figure by another, for example, current assets to current liabilities. Ratio of one figure expressed as number of times of the other like inventory turnover (times in a year). Percentage is a special type of ratio which expresses the relation in hundredth *e.g.*, gross profit is 20 per cent on sales.

A ratio by itself tells us nothing. If for example, the gross profit of M/s ABC LTD this year is 19 per cent, can it be called good? In order to get some meaningful result, this figure is to be compared with some other ratio. Firstly, this may be compared to the previous year or years' rate of gross profit. This rate may be compared to an industry average in the absence of previous years' records. However, if the firm happens to be a monopoly firm or if the other ratios are not available, there are accounting norms with which a comparison can be made.

Analysis of financial statements may be carried out by a number of groups such as creditors short-term and long-term, equity owners, investors, management and institutions like banks including development banks. Accordingly, there may be different types of ratios.

TYPES OF RATIOS

Some important ratio used for financial analyses are:

- Liquidity Ratios
- Activity Ratios
- Profitability Ratios
- Leverage Ratios
- Other Ratios.

ANALYSIS OF SHORT-TERM CREDITORS

The short-term creditors are people who are interested mainly in short-term solvency *i.e.*, company's ability to pay off its short-term obligations.

To judge short-term liquidity two ratios are generally calculated: current ratio and quick ratio.

1. Current Ratio and Quick Ratio

Current Ratio:

It is calculated by dividing current assets by current liabilities.

$$\text{The formula is Current Ratio} = \left(\frac{\text{Current Assets}}{\text{Current Liabilities}}\right)$$

This ratio shows the margin of current assets over current liabilities which shows company's strength to pay its creditors.

The current assets to be included generally are: cash, bank, inventory, accounts receivables including bills receivables, short-term investments, prepaid expenses and the like.

Current liabilities include accounts payable as well as bills payable, expenses outstanding, bank overdraft, and other short-term borrowings.

The accounting norm for this ratio is 2 : 1, *i.e.*, if the current assets are twice as large as the current liabilities, the liquidity position is considered to be satisfactory.

However, this ratio is not a very dependent indicator of short-term solvency as it is susceptible to window dressing. A week before the final closing of accounts the management observes that its current ratio is 1.5 : 1 *i.e.*,

$$\left(\frac{\text{CA}}{\text{CL}} = \frac{₹\,9,00,000}{₹\,6,00,000}\right).$$

It decides to pay off ₹ 4,00,000 to its creditors just before the final closing the ratio improves to 2.5 : 1 *i.e.*,

$$\left(\frac{\text{CA}}{\text{CL}} = \frac{₹\,5,00,000}{₹\,2,00,000}\right)$$

Quick ratio:

The ratio is calculated by the formula.

$$\text{Quick Ratio} = \frac{\text{Quick Assets}}{\text{Current Liabilities}}$$

Quick current assets are cash, bank, debtors and bills receivables (inventory and prepared expenses are excluded). Quick Ratio of 1 : 1 is considered satisfactory.

Both the above given ratios are based on balance sheet figures that give the position of a company on a particular date only. The management is more interested in the events as they happen throughout the year for which **activity** ratios are calculated.

2. Activity Ratios

Under this category are included ratios like: Inventory-Turnover, Assets-Turnover, Debtors-Turnover, Capital-Turnover etc.

(*i*) **Inventory Turnover:**

The liquidity of a firm's inventory may be calculated by dividing the cost of goods sold by the firm's inventory.

$$\textbf{Inventory Turnover} = \frac{\text{Cost of goods sold}}{\text{Average inventory}}$$

Cost of goods sold can be calculated by sales minus gross profit or opening stock + purchases + wages + direct expenses minus closing stock.

Average inventory may be calculated by adding opening inventory and closing inventory and divided by 2.

High turnover ratio may indicate that the firm may lose sales in future if it fails to deliver the goods on time. A low inventory turnover results from **excessive inventory** being carried by the firm. It my cause high cost of carrying inventory.

(*ii*) **Assets Turnover:**

It is calculated by dividing sales (alternatively cost of sales) by the firm's assets (alternatively total assets or operating assets). This ratio measures the efficiency with which assets are utilized. It also serves as a test of adequacy of sales. This is expressed at times (10 times or 12 times, etc.)

Suppose Net Sales of ABC Co. are ₹ 50,00,000 and its fixed assets are ₹ 5,00,000 while the ratio of gross profit is 20%, fixed assets turnover will be

$$= \left(\frac{\text{Sales} - \text{GP}}{\text{Fixed Assets}}\right)$$

$$= \frac{50,00,000 - 10,00,000}{5,00,000} = \frac{40,00,000}{5,00,000} = 8 \text{ times}$$

$$\text{Alternatively} = \frac{50,00,000}{5,00,000} = 10 \text{ times} \left(\frac{\text{Sales}}{\text{Fixed Assets}}\right).$$

(*iii*) **Debtors Turnover:**

Debtors in this context include accounts receivables, bills receivables that are on account of goods sold on credit.

$$\text{Debtors turnover} = \frac{\text{Net credit sales}}{\text{Average debtors}}$$

Average debtors will be calculated by dividing the sum of opening and closing figures of debtors by 2.

Average collection period or debt collection period can be calculated by a simple formula:

$$= \left(\frac{\text{360 or 365}}{\text{Debtors turnover}}\right)$$

Alternatively, it can be calculated by:

$$\text{Average collection period} = \frac{\text{Average debtors}}{\text{Credit sales}} \times \text{Period of sales (365)}$$

If the data pertains to a year, 365 or 360 days may be taken. This ratio helps the financial manager to ascertain the efficiency with which book debts are utilized or collected. Higher days of collection period indicates more costs and increased risk.

3. Profitability Ratios

Profitability can be studied in two ways. *Firstly*, profits related to sales, and *Secondly*, profits related to investment. In the first category Gross Profit Ratio and Net Profit Ratio can be calculated in the following manner:

(*i*) *Gross profit ratio*

$$= \frac{\text{Gross profit}}{\text{Sales}} \times 100$$

Gross profit ratio is very significant as a fall in this ratio would put management to difficulty since all overhead expenses are met out of gross profits.

(ii) *Net profit ratio*

$$= \frac{\text{Net profit}}{\text{Sales}} \times 100$$

Similarly, net profit ratio tells us the rate of profits on sales. Steady rate or increasing rate shows managerial efficiency.

(iii) *Return on equity share capital*

Another important ratio can be calculated by relating profit after tax to capital employed.

$$\text{R.O. Equity} = \frac{\text{PAT} - \text{Preference Share Dividend}}{\text{Equity Capital}}$$

where PAT means profit after tax.

This ratio is an indicator of managerial effectiveness in running the company.

(iv) *Return on investment*

Another method used for calculating this ratio is called return on investment, (ROI). This is one of the key ratios. If one is allowed to calculate only one ratio and comment on the profitability of the company, this ratio would be sufficient to tell about the company's performance.

$$\text{ROI} = \frac{\text{Profit}}{\text{Sales}} \times \frac{\text{Sales}}{\text{Capital employed}}$$

$$\text{Hence} = \frac{\text{Profit}}{\text{Capital employed}}$$

where capital employed would mean Net Fixed Assets plus Net Working Capital = (Current Assets minus Current Liabilities).

This ratio indicates company's earning power. This ratio can be represented by a chart called DU Pont. Chart (as it was first used by M/s DU pont of USA) as given in Fig. 3.1.

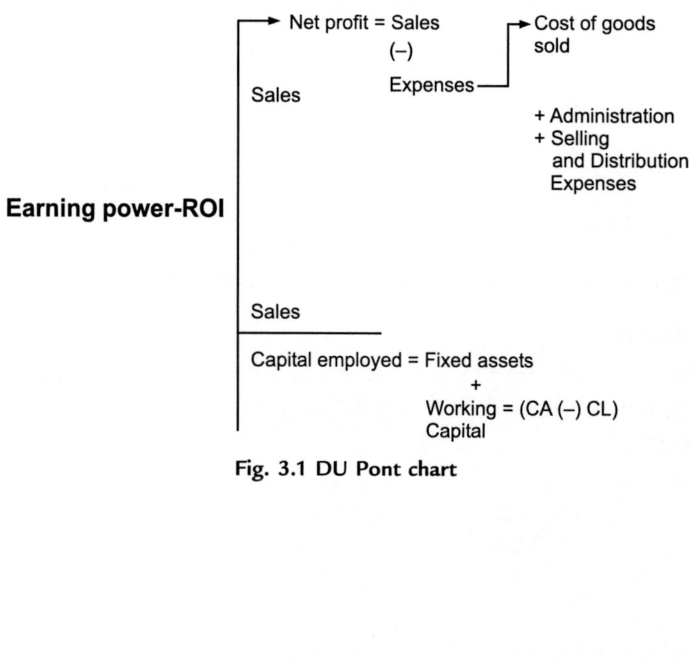

Fig. 3.1 DU Pont chart

4. Leverage Ratios

Leverage ratios which measure the contribution of owners with the finance provided by the firm's creditors, have a number of implications such as:

(*i*) Creditors (debenture holders, depositors, etc.) look to equity capital which serves as a margin of safety of them.

(*ii*) Returns to the owners get magnified due to use of debt (advantages of favourable leverage or trading on equity). (*Ref. Chapter 2: Long-term Finance and Capital Structure*).

Ratio calculated in this category are:

(*i*) Debt = Equity Ratio

$$DE = \frac{\text{Long-term Debt}}{\text{Shareholder's Equity}}$$

Debt here means long-term borrowing by way of debentures, term loans of public deposits excluding current liabilities. Shareholder's equity capital plus preference capital. A better measure to calculate debt equity ratio is:

$$DE = \frac{\text{Total Debt}}{\text{Shareholder's Equity}}$$

Total debt here includes long-term debt plus current liabilities.

A high debt equity ratio has implications such as low margin of safety for creditors, future debt raising capacity not available. Fixed obligations by way of interest and replayment of principal.

(*ii*) Interest Coverage Ratio

Another ratio calculated for leverage is interest coverage ratio which is calculated as:

$$\text{Interest Coverage} = \frac{\text{EBIT}}{\text{I}}$$

EBIT means earnings before Interest and Taxes, and 'I' means Interest charge.

This ratio indicates company's strength in meeting its interest obligations. Too high a ratio means under utilization of debt and too low means risk of using excessive debt.

5. Other Ratios

(*i*) **Operating ratio is calculated by the formula:**

Cost of goods sold + Other operating Expenses, like administrable selling and distribution expenses.

Cost of Goods Sold + Operating Expenses

Cost of goods sold is (Opening stock plus Purchases plus Direct expenses minus closing stock) OR it may be simply: Sales minus Gross Profit.

(*ii*) $\frac{\text{Dividend}}{\text{Yield}} = \text{D.Y. Ratio } \frac{\text{Dividend per shares}}{\text{Mkt. Price per share}} \times 100$

This tells the true return to an investor on high investment.

(*iii*) **EPS = Earning per share is calculated by:**

$$EPS = \frac{\text{Net Profit available to Equity}}{\text{Number of Equity floated}}$$

DPS: Dividend Per Share can be calculated by

$$= \frac{\text{Dividend amount}}{\text{No. of Equity shares}}$$

(*iv*) **P/E Price earning ratio:**

It is calculated by dividing the market price of a share by the EPS. P/E ratio tells us the price currently being paid for each rupee of currently reported earnings per share.

Higher the P/E, the better it is for owners.

Illustration 3.3

Following is the Profit and Loss Account and a Balance Sheet of M/s John Ltd.

You are required to:

(*a*) Redraft them for the purpose of analysis, and

(*b*) Calculate:

(*i*) Gross Profit Ratio

(*ii*) Overall Profitability Ratio

(*iii*) Current Ratio

(*iv*) Equity Debt Ratio

(*v*) Stock Turnover Ratio

(*vi*) Liquidity Ratio.

M/s JGR Management Research Ltd., Mumbai
Profit and Loss Account

(₹ in '000)

Particular	Amount	Particular	Amount
Opening Stock		Sales	1,000
– Raw Materials	50	Closing stock	
– Finished Goods	100	– Raw Material	150
Purchases of Raw Material	300	– Finished Goods	100
Wages	200	Profit on Sale of Shares	50
Manufacturing Expenses	100		
Administrative Expenses	50		
Selling and Distribution Expenses	50		
Loss on Sale of plant	55		
Interest on Debentures	10		
Net Profit	385		
	1,300		**1,300**

M/s JGR Management Research Ltd., Mumbai
Balance Sheet

(₹ in '000)

Liabilities	Amount	Assets	Amount
Share capital			
– Equity	100	Fixed Assets	250
– Preference	100	Stock of Raw material	150
Reserve and Surplus	100	Finished Goods	100
Debentures	200	Sundry Debtors	100
Sundry Creditors	100	Bank	50
Bills Payable	50		
	650		**650**

Solution:

(*a*) **Redrafted Statements**

M/s JGR Management Research Ltd. Mumbai
Income Statement

Particulars		Details	Amount
Sales			₹ **10,00,000**
Less: Cost of Sales:			
Raw materials consumed		₹ 2,00,000	
(Op. Stock + Purchases – Closing stock)			
i.e., (50,000 + 3,00,000 – 1,50,000)			
Direct wages		₹ 2,00,000	
Manufacturing expenses		1,00,000	
∴ Cost of production		**5,00,000**	
Add: Opening stock of finished goods		1,00,000	
		6,00,000	
Less: Closing stock of finished goods		1,00,000	₹ 5,00,000
Gross Profit			₹ 5,00,000
Less: Operating expenses:			
Administration expenses	₹ 50,000		
Selling and distribution expenses	₹ 50,000		₹ 1,00,000
Net Operating Profit			₹ **4,00,000**
Add: Non-trading income:			
Profit on sale of shares			₹ 50,000
			₹ 4,50,000
Less: Non-trading expenses or losses:			
Loss on sale of plant			₹ 55,000
Income before interest and tax			₹ 3,95,000
Less: Interest on debentures			₹ 10,000
Net Profit before tax as per Profit and Loss Account			₹ **3,85,000**

Operating Ratio in this case is:

$$= 100 \times \frac{\text{Cost of goods sold} + \text{Administration Exp.} + \text{Selling and Distribution Exp.}}{\text{Sales}}$$

$$= 100 \times \frac{5,00,000 + 50,000 + 50,000}{10,00,000}$$

$$= 60\%$$

M/s JGR Management Research Ltd., Mumbai

Balance Sheet (or Position Statement)

Particular		Amount in ₹
Bank balance		50,000
Sundry debtors		1, 40,000
Liquid Assets or Quick Assets		**1,50,000**
Inventories:		
Stock of raw materials		1,50,000
Stock of finished goods		1,00,000
Current assets:	(*a*)	**4,00,000**
Sundry creditors		1,00,000
Bills payable		50,000
Current liabilities	(*b*)	**1,50,000**
Working capital CA – CL = (*a* – *b*) (₹ 4,00,000 – ₹ 1, 50,000)		2,50,000
Add: Fixed assests		2,50,000
Capital employed		**5,00,000**
Less: Debentures		2,00,000
Shareholders' net worth or share holders' Funds		3,00,000
Less: Preference share capital		1,00,000
Equity **shareholder's** net worth		2,00,000
Represented by equity share capital		1,00,000
Reserves		1,00,000
		2,00,000

(*b*) **Calculation of Ratios**

(*i*) Gross Profit Ratio:

$$= \frac{\text{Gross profit}}{\text{Sales}} \times 100 \quad = \frac{5,00,000}{10,00,000} \times 100 = 50\%$$

(*ii*) Overall Profitability Ratio:

$$= \frac{\text{Operating profit}}{\text{Capital employed}} \times 100 = \frac{4,00,000}{5,00,000} \times 100 = 80\%$$

(*iii*) Current Ratio:

$$= \frac{\text{Current assets}}{\text{Current liabilities}} = \frac{4,00,000}{1,50,000} = 2.67 : 1$$

(*iv*) Debt-Equity Ratio:

$$= \frac{\text{External equities}}{\text{Internal equities}} = \frac{3,50,000}{3,00,000} = 1.17 : 1$$

$$= \frac{\text{Total long – term debt}}{\text{Total long – term funds}} = \frac{2,00,000}{5,00,000} = 0.40$$

OR

$$= \frac{\text{Total long – term debt}}{\text{Shareholders funds}} = \frac{2,00,000}{3,00,000} = 0.67$$

(*v*) Stock turnover ratio:

(*a*) As regards average total inventory

$$= \frac{\text{Cost of goods sold}}{\text{Average Inventory}} \qquad = \frac{5,00,000}{2,00,000} = 2.5$$

(of raw materials as well as finished goods)

(*b*) As regards average inventory of finished goods:

$$= \frac{\text{Cost of goods sold}}{\text{Average Inventory of finished goods}} \qquad = \frac{5,00,000}{1,00,000} = 5$$

(*c*) As regards average inventory of raw materials:

$$= \frac{\text{Materials consumed}}{\text{Average inventory of raw materials}} \qquad = \frac{2,00,000}{1,00,000} = 2$$

(*vi*) Liquidity Ratio or Quick Ratio or Acid Test Ratio.

$$= \frac{\text{Liquid Assets}}{\text{Current Liabilities}} \qquad = \frac{1,50,000}{1,50,000} = 1:1$$

Illustration 3.4

You are provided with the following figures of two companies from which you are required to calculate the operating, financial and combined leverages.

Particulars	DCM Ltd. (₹ in lakhs)	BCM Ltd. (₹ in lakhs)
Sales	500	1,000
Variable costs	200	300
Contribution	300	700
Fixed costs	150	400
EBIT	150	300
Interest	50	100
Profit before tax	100	200

Solution:

Determination of operating, financial and combined leverages

Particulars	DCM Ltd. (₹ in lakhs)	BCM Ltd. (₹ in lakhs)
Sales	500	1,000
Less: variable costs	200	300
Contribution	300	700
Fixed costs	150	400
EBIT	150	300
Less: interest	50	100
EBT	100	200
DOL (contribution/EBIT)	2	2.33
DFL (EBIT/EBT)	1.5	1.5
DCL (DOL × DFL)	3	3.5

Illustration 3.5

In a meeting held at Solan towards the end of previous year, the Directors of M/s Vedanta Ltd. have taken a decision to diversify. At present Vedanta Ltd. sells all finished goods from its own warehouse. The company issued debentures on 01.01.201? (current year) and purchased Fixed Assets on the same day. The purchase prices have remained stable during the concened period. Following information is provided to you.

M/s Vedanta Ltd.
Income Statement

Particulars	Previous year ₹		Current year ₹	
Cash Sales	30,000		32,000	
Credit Sales	2,70,000	3,00,000	3,42,000	3,74,000
Less: Cost of goods sold		2,36,000		2,98,000
Gross profit		64,000		76,000
Less: Expenses				
Warehousing	13,000		14,000	
Transport	6,000		10,000	
Administrative and Selling	19,000		19,000	
Interest on Debenture	11,000		14,000	
		49,000	2,000	59,000
Net Profit		**15,000**		**17,000**

M/s Vedanta Ltd.
Balance Sheet

Particulars	Previous year ₹		Current year ₹	
Fixed Assets (Net Block)	–	30,000	–	40,000
Debtors	50,000		82,000	
Cash at Bank	10,000		7,000	
Stock	60,000		94,000	
Total Current Assets (CA)	**1,20,000**		**1,83,000**	
Creditors	50,000		76,000	
Total Current Liabilities (CL)	50,000		76,000	
Working Capital (CA – CL)	70,000		1,07,000	
Total Assets	**1,00,000**		**1,47,000**	
Represented by:				
Share Capital	75,000		75,000	
Reserve and Surplus	25,000		42,000	
Debentures	–		30,000	
	1,00,000		**1,47,000**	

Solution:

M/s Vedanta Ltd.
Calculation of Ratios

	Previous year	Current year
1. Gross profit ratio		
$= \frac{\textit{Gross profit}}{\textit{sales}}$	$= \frac{64,000 \times 100}{3,00,000}$	$= \frac{76,000 \times 100}{3,74,000}$
	= 21.3%	= 20.3
2. Operating expense to sales ratio		
$= \frac{\textit{Operating exp}}{\textit{Total sales}}$	$= \frac{49,000 \times 100}{3,00,000}$	$= \frac{57,000 \times 100}{3,74,000}$
	= 16.3%	= 15.2%
3. Operating profit ratio		
$= \frac{\textit{Operating profit}}{\textit{Total sales}}$	$= \frac{15,000 \times 100}{3,00,000}$	$= \frac{19,000 \times 100}{3,74,000}$
	= 5%	= 5.08%
4. Capital turnover ratio		
$= \frac{\textit{Sales}}{\textit{Capital employed}}$	$= \frac{3,00,000}{1,00,000}$	$= \frac{3,74,000}{1,47,000}$
	= 3	= 2.54
5. Stock turnover ratio		
$= \frac{\textit{COGS}}{\textit{Average stock}}$	$= \frac{2,36,000}{50,000}$	$= \frac{2,98,000}{77,000}$
	= 4.7	= 3.9
6. Net Profit to Network		
$= \frac{\textit{Net profit}}{\textit{Networth}}$	$= \frac{15,000 \times 100}{1,00,000}$	$= \frac{17,000 \times 100}{1,17,000}$
	= 15%	= 14.5%
7. Debtors collection period		
$= \frac{\textit{Average debtors}}{\textit{Average daily sales}}$	$= \frac{50,000}{739.73}$	$= \frac{82,000}{936.99}$
(Refer to working note)	= 67.6 days	= 87.5 days
Working note:		
Average daily sales $= \frac{\textit{Credit sales}}{365}$	$= \frac{2,70,000}{365}$	$= \frac{3,42,000}{365}$
	= ₹ 739.73	= ₹ 936.99

Analysis:

The decline in the Gross profit ratio could be either due to a reduction in the selling price or increase in the direct expenses (since the purchase price has remained the same). Similarly there is a decline in the ratio of Operating expenses to Sales. However since Operating expenses have little bearing with sales, a decline in this ratio cannot be necessarily be interpreted as an increase in operational efficiency. An indepth analysis reveals that the decline in the warehousing and the administrative expenses has been partly set off by an increase in the transport and the selling expenses. The operating profit ratio has remained the same in spite of a decline in the Gross profit margin ratio. In fact the company has not benefited at all in terms of operational performance because of the increased sales.

The company has not been able to deploy its capital efficiently. This is indicated by a decline in the Capital turnover from 3 to 2.5 times. In case the capital turnover would have remained at 3 the company would have increased Sales and Profits by ₹ 67,000 and ₹ 3,350 respectively.

The decline in the Stock Turnover ratio implies that the company has increased its investment in stock. Return on Networth has declined indicating that the additional capital employed has failed to increase the volume of sales proportionately. The increase in the Average collection period indicates that the company has become liberal in extending credit on sales. However, there is a corresponding increase in the current assets due to such a policy.

It appears as if the decision to expand the business has not shown the desired results.

REVIEW QUESTIONS

1. (*a*) What do you mean by the term "Analysis of Financial statement?
   (*b*) What are the tools used for the purpose?
   (*c*) Explain in this context the main ratios you would like to calculate for judging liquidity, profitability, activity and leverage.
2. Explain the utility of ROI (Return on Investment) as a single ratio to judge company's performance.
3. Write notes on:
   (*a*) Profitability ratios
   (*b*) Leverage ratios
4. Differentiate between comparative statement and common size statement.

Chapter 4

FUND FLOW STATEMENTS AND CASH FLOW STATEMENTS

Most of the business firms whether big or small do prepare the financial statements namely income statement (to know the profit or loss) and balance sheet (to ascertain the financial position) at the year end. Although these financial statements provide very useful information on various aspects such as growth pattern, current status of the firm, yet they do not answer an important question concerning where from the firm received funds and how the firm spent those. For example, it is heard from a business man that, "I have no cash even though my profit and loss account shows a profit of ₹ 2,00,000." Thus, the two statements (income statements and balance sheet) do not reveal causes of changes in assets and liabilities of a firm as given in the two consecutive balance sheets! A Funds flow statement answers these questions. This is the reason why most of the modern enterprises prepare a Funds Flow Statement over and above the other legally required Financial Statements.

MEANING OF 'FUNDS', 'FLOW' AND 'FUNDS FLOW STATEMENT'

Funds:

Though the term 'Funds' has variety of meanings yet in the present context it refers to the Net working capital, *i.e.*, different between current assets and current liabilities.

Current assets are the assets acquired for the purpose of converting them into cash by selling them or by using them in the production process. Broadly speaking current assets are cash, bank, accounts receivables including bills receivables, inventory, *i.e.*, raw material, work in progress and finished goods, short-term securities or investments, prepaid expenses or unexpired insurance.

Illustration 4.1

Differenciate between Current Assets and Current Liabilities from the following information of M/s Universal Tech Ltd. Kolkata by preparing an imaginary balance sheet.

Solution:

Balance Sheets of M/s Universal Tech Ltd. Kolkata

as on 31.12.201?... (Pervious year) and 31.12.201?... (Current year)

Liabilities	Pervious year	Current year	Assets	Pervious year	Current year
Fixed or Non-current Liabilities			Fixed Assets		
Capital: Equity, Debentures, Long-term Loans etc.	12,00,000	15,00,000	Building, Plant, Machinery etc.	10,00,000	12,00,000
Current Liabilities			**Current Assets**		
Accounts Payable			Cash		
Bank Overdraft	10,00,000	12,00,000	Bank		
Bills Payable			Debtors	12,00,000	15,00,000
Expenses Due			Bills Receivable		
			Short-term Securities		
			Inventories		
			Prepaid Exp.		
Total	**22,00,000**	**27,00,000**		**22,00,000**	**27,00,000**

Fund at the end to previous year = Current assets – Current liabilities = 12,00,000 – 10,00,000 = 2,00,000, and

at the end of current year = current assets – current liabilities = 15,00,000 – 12,00,000 = 3,00,000

Current Liabilities

Current liabilities are these obligations that are to be paid off within the current financial year. However, the more fact that it is to be discharged within the current year does not make it a current liability unless it is payable out of current assets or by creation of current liabilities. For example debentures maturing for repayment in the current year will not be formed as current liability as these are to be paid out of the fresh issue of shares or debentures or from profits.

Flow

The term 'flow' means either increase or decrease in the funds. If by a transaction the working capital position improves over what is was earlier, it is said to have caused inflow of funds and vice-versa. In the foregoing balance sheet, it is clearly noticeable that the non-current liabilities increased from ₹ 12,00,000 to ₹ 15,00,000 which has caused 'inflow' of funds amounting to ₹ 3,00,000. On the other hand, the fixed assets increased from ₹ 10,00,000 to ₹ 12,00,000 which means an outflow of funds by ₹ 2,00,000.

Funds Flow Statement

A statement that shows the various sources and uses of funds explaining the reasons for net increase of decrease in working capital (funds) is called a Funds Flow Statement.

Uses of Funds Flow Statement

A Funds Flow Statement helps the analyst to understand the financial statements in a better way. It provides a ready answer to a large number of questions:

1. Where did the profits go?
2. Why were the dividends not larger then even though there had been good profits?
3. How was it possible to give higher dividends much is excess of current year earnings?
4. How was the purchase of new plant financed?
5. What happened to the proceeds received from the sale of plant/building?
6. What became of the money received from the issue of debentures, shares or money received from institutions?
7. How was working capital increases financed?

Thus, the funds flow statement helps management in managing working capital effectively. It helps management in having a better control over funds. When a Performa or Budgeted Flow Statement is prepared, it helps management in identifying the gaps in flows.

Before we attempt a few numericals to explain the concept of Fund Flow Statement, it would be appropriate to study the concept of Cash Flow Statement and the difference between the Cash Flow and Funds Flow Statements.

Cash Flow Statement

It is not very much different from a Funds Flow Statements except that in the former we strictly restrict ourselves to sources and uses of cash alone. The Cash Flow Statement explains the causes for a change in the cash position of the firm while Funds Flow Statement explains the reasons for changes in working capital which includes cash and bank balances.

Difference between Funds Flow Statement and Cash Flow Statement:

1. Cash Flow Analysis is more useful as a tool for short-term solvency or liquidity than Funds Low Analysis as the funds may increase without improvement in real liquidity position. For example, the stock may increases or debtors may increase due to non-recovery but the two may not be easily realized in cash.
2. Cash Flow Statement is concerned with cash only whereas Funds Flow is concerned with total working capital and it changes during two balance sheet dates.
3. Cash Flow Statement though provides useful information but it tells only about the movement of cash whereas Funds Flow Statements tells us about all the components of working capital.
4. An improvement in working capital need not mean increase in cash whereas increase in cash necessarily means increase liquidity and working capital.
5. Funds Flow Statements funds do not get affected due to change in current assets and current liabilities, *i.e.*, a change in current assets and correspondingly in current liability does not affect funds. Payment to creditors for example, has the effect of reducing current liabilities as well as current assets—leaving the funds position the same as before.

Major Sources and Uses of Funds

"Funds" have many sources and it can be for different purposes. Following are some of the major sources and uses of funds:

Sources and Uses

Issue of shares, debentures and raising of long-term loans. Raising of long-term funds in cash is a source. If, however, shares or debentures are issued for consideration other than cash or current assets it would not cause flow of funds. For example, if building is acquired for ₹ 5,00,000 and shares worth ₹ 5,00,000 are issued to vendors, it would not be a source of funds.

Proceeds from the sale of long-term or non-current assets. The net proceeds whether less than or more than the book value of the assets like plant, machinery, buildings etc. form a source. Uses of funds include purchase of assets, loan recovered drawings etc.

Funds From Operations

Funds from operations happens to be a recurring source. The usual method of calculating funds from operations is:

Net profit as given in the profit and loss account.

Add:

Items that do not constitute outflow of funds such as:

(*i*) Depreciation written off
(*ii*) Goodwill written off
(*iii*) Preliminary expenses written off
(*iv*) Discount written off
(*v*) Loss on sale of non-current assets

Less:

Gain on sale of any fixed asset etc.

Let us take an example to show how Fund from Operation is calculated.

Illustration 4.2

Calculate Fund from Operation from the following information:

M/s ABC Ltd., New Delhi
Profit and Loss Account
for the year ending

(Amount in ₹)

Particular		Amount	Particular	Amount
To Stock		80,000	By sales	25,00,000
To Purchases	1,00,000			
Less: Returns	20,000	80,000	By stock	2,00,000
To Wages	50,000			
Add: Outstanding	25,000	75,000		
To Gross profit		24,65,000		
		27,00,000		**27,00,000**
To Rent		24,000	By Gross Profit	24,65,000
To Salary	75,000			
Less: Prepaid	12,500	62,500		
To Dep. on furniture		7,500		
To Discount on issue of shares		25,000		
To Goodwill written off		12,500		
To Preliminary Exp.		15,000		
To Net profit		23,18,500		
		24,65,000		**24,65,000**

Solution:

Now, Net Profit as revealed by Income Statement is ₹ 23,18,500 but is it the same as funds flow operations? If all transactions were strictly on cash basis, it would have been Funds From Operations. But it is not so, as we observe there are some transactions such as depreciation on furniture, discount on issue of shares, goodwill written off etc. which are merely adjustment, *i.e.*, these are treated as expense for the purpose of ascertaining taxable net profits but they do not constitute an outflow of funds. As such funds from operations can be calculated in the following manner:

Funds from Operation

Particular		Amount
Net profit as revealed by Profit and Loss A/c.		₹ 23,18,500
Add: Non-fund items:		
Preliminary expenses	₹ 15,000	
Goodwill written off	12,500	
Discount of issue of shares	25,000	
Depreciation on furniture	7,500	60,000
Funds from operations		**23,78,500**

Preparation of a Funds Flow Statement

Before an attempt is made to prepare a statement called Sources and Uses of Funds or simply a Funds Flow Statement, it is important to prepare a Schedule of Change in the Working Capital.

Performa for Schedule of Change in Working Capital

1	2	3	4		5	
Assets and Liabilities	Figures for beginning of the period	Figures for end of the period	Changes in current item		Changes in non-current items	
			4(a) CA↑ CL↓	4(b) CA↓ CL↑	5(a) NCA↑ NCL↓	5(b) NCA↓ NCL↑

1. Column 4 is meant to record changes in current items, *i.e.*, current assets and current liabilities.
2. Col. 4(*a*) will record increase in current assets and decrease in current liabilities.
3. Col. 4(*b*) will record increase in current liabilities and decrease in current assets. Since increase in current assets and decrease in current liabilities both cause working capital to increase, it can also be termed as 'increase in working capital' and extending the same logic column 5 can be called 'decrease in working capital'. The net different between the two will be termed as net increase or net decrease in working capital.

4. Col. 5 is meant to record changes in non-current items *i.e.,* Fixed Assets and Fixed Liabilities.
5. Column 5(*a*) would record increase in fixed Assets and decrease in Long-term liabilities and it would show uses of funds while column 5(*b*) would record increase in non-current liabilities and decrease in non-current assets which would mean sources of funds.

   The difference in column 4 must be equal to the difference in column 5.

Illustration 4.3

From the following Balance Sheets of M/s Mount Everest Corporation, Kolkata, prepare a Schedule of Changes in Working Capital and a Statement of Funds Flow:

Balance Sheet

as on 31.12.201?... (Pervious year) and 31.12.201?... (Current year)

(Amount in ₹)

Liabilities	Pervious Year	Current Year	Assets	Previous Year	Current Year
Capital	1,60,000	1,70,000	Land and Bldg.	1,00,000	1,00,000
P and L A/c	29,000	49,000	Plant	48,000	68,000
Creditors	18,000	10,000	Stock	18,000	14,000
Mortgage Loan	–	10,000	Debtors	33,000	39,000
			Cash at Bank	8,000	18,000
	2,07,000	**2,39,000**		**2,07,000**	**2,39,000**

Solution:

M/s Mount Everest Corporation, Kolkata

Schedule of Changes in Working Capital

(Amount in ₹)

1	2	3	4		5	
Particulars	**Previous year**	**Current year**	**Changes in Current**		**Changes in non-current items**	
			4(a)	**4(b)**	**5(a)**	**5(b)**
			Increase	**Decreases**	**Increases**	**Decreases**
Liabilities						
Capital	1,60,000	1,70,000				10,000
Profit and Loss A/c	29,000	49,000				20,000
Creditors	18,000	10,000	8,000			
Mortgage Loan	–	10,000				10,000
Assets						
Land and Bldg.	1,00,000	1,00,000	–			
Plant	48,000	68,000			20,000	
Stock	18,000	14,000		4,000		
Debtors	33,000	39,000	6,000			
Cash at Bank	8,000	18,000	10,000			
			24,000	4,000	20,000	40,000
Net Increase in Working Capital				**20,000**	**20,000**	
			24,000	24,000	40,000	40,000

M/s Mount Everest Corporation, Kolkata
Statement of Funds Flow

Particular	Amount ₹
Source of Founds:	
Issue of capital	₹ 10,000
Provided by profits	20,000
Raised form loan	10,000
	40,000
Application:	
Purchase of plant	20,000
Increase in W/capital	**₹ 20,000**

CASH FLOW ANALYSIS

A Cash Flow Statement is used for short-term financial analysis. Every business firm needs as to pull off its maturing obligations. When it is prepared based on future projections, it helps us in identifying gaps in inflow and outflow. The main advantages of a Cash Flow Statement are:

1. **Efficient utilisation of cash:** A projected cash flow prepared in advance can help management in planning and coordinating business activities to use cash effectively. If it finds idle funds, the same can be lent for short period and if there is shortage, short-term borrowings may be arranged.
2. **Internal financial management:** Cash from operations once known, can be used in paying off long-term borrowings or some policy decisions can be effectively formulated. Such policies may be dividend policy, capital budgeting etc.

BASIS OF COMPARISON OF PERFORMANCE

When projected cash flow statement is compared with the actual one, it is easy to know why the deficiency or variation has happened. If recovery from debtors has gone slow, action can be taken to remedy the problem.

PREPARATION OF CASH FLOW STATEMENT

Illustration 4.4

Balance sheet of M/s Amresh and M/s Biresh Pvt. Ltd. as on 1.1.201?... and 31.12.201?... were as follows:

M/s Amresh and M/s Biresh Chennai
Balance Sheet
as on.... 1.1.201? to 31.12.201?...

(Amount in ₹)

Liabilities	Pervious Year	Current Year	Assets	Pervious Year	Current Year
Creditors	40,000	44,000	Cash	10,000	7,000
Mrs. Amresh	25,000	—	Debtors	30,000	50,000
Loan			Stock	35,000	25,000
Loan from Bank	40,000	50,000	Machinery	80,000	55,000
			Land	40,000	50,000
Capital	1,25,000	1,53,000	Building	35,000	60,000
	2,30,000	**2,47,000**		**2,30,000**	**2,47,000**

During the year a machine costing ₹ 10,000 (accumulated depreciation ₹ 3,000) was sold for ₹ 5,000. The provisions for depreciation against machinery as on 1.1.201?... (beginning of previous year) was ₹ 25,000 and on 31.12.201?... (end of previous year) ₹ 40,000. Net profit for the previous year amounted to ₹ 45,000. You are required to prepare a Cash Flow Statement.

Solution:

M/s Amresh and Biresh Pvt. Ltd., Chennai
Cash Flow Statement
as on 1.1.201?...

Particular	Details	Amount
Cash Balance as on 1.1.201?... (Beginning of previous year)		₹ 10,000
Add: **Sources**		
Cash from Operations	₹ 59,000	
Loan from Bank	₹ 10,000	
Sale of Machinery	₹ 5,000	₹ 74,000
		₹ 84,000
Less: **Applications**		
Purchase of Land	₹ 10,000	
Purchase of Building	₹ 25,000	
Mrs. Amit Loan repaid	₹ 25,000	
Drawings	₹ 17,000	₹ 77,000
Cash balance as on Dec. 31.201?... (End of previous year)		**₹ 7,000**

Working Notes:

(*i*) Cash from Operations:

Profit made during the year		₹ 45,000
Add: Depreciation on machinery	₹ 18,000	
Loss on sale of machinery	₹ 2,000	
Decrease in stock	₹ 10,000	
Increase in creditors	₹ 4,000	₹ 34,000
		₹ 79,000
Less: Increase in Debtors		₹ 20,000
Cash from Operations		**₹ 59,000**

Machinery Account

Particular	Amount	Particular	Amount
To Balance b/d	1,05,000	By Bank	5,000
		By Loss on sale of machinery	2,000
		By Provision for depreciation	3,000
		By Balance c/d	95,000
	1,05,000		**1,05,000**

Provision for Depreciation Account

Particular	Amount	Particular	Amount
To Machinery A/c	3,000	By Balance b/d	25,000
To Balance c/d	40,000	By P & L A/c	
		(Depreciation charged balancing figure)	18,000
	43,000		**43,000**

Illustration 4.5

The financial position of M/s Devashish International Ltd., Mussoorie as on Jan. 1 and December 31, 201?... was as follows:

M/s Devashish International Ltd., Mussoorie
Balance Sheet
as on....31, 201?

Liabilities	Ist Jan. (₹)	31st Dec. (₹)	Assets	1st Jan. (₹)	31st Dec. (₹)
Current Liabilities for Goods	36,000	40,600	Cash	4,000	3,600
Mrs. Devashish Loan	–	20,000	Debtors	35,000	38,000
Loan from Bank	30,000	25,000	Stock	25,000	22,000
Hire-purchase Vendor	–	20,000	Land	20,000	30,000
Capital	1,48,000	1,54,000	Buildings	50,000	55,000
			Machinery	80,000	86,000
			Delivery Van	–	25,000
	2,14,000	**2,59,600**		**2,14,000**	**2,59,600**

The delivery van was purchased in December 201?... (end of the year) on hire purchase basis, a payment of ₹ 5,000 was made immediately and the balance of the amount is to be paid in 20 monthly installments of ₹ 1,000 each together with interest @ 12% p.a. During the year partners withdrew ₹ 26,000 for domestic expenditure. The provision for depreciation against machinery on 31.12. 200? (12 year ago) was ₹ 27,000 and on 31.12. 201?... (after one year) was ₹ 36,000.

You are required to prepare:

(*a*) the Cash Flow Statement, and

(*b*) Show the Funds Flow Statement.

Solution: (*a*)

Schedule of Changes in Working Capital
M/s Devashish International Ltd., Mussoorie

(Amount in ₹)

Particular	Changes in current items		Changes in non-current items	
	Increase	Decrease	Increase	Decrease
Cash		400		
Debtors	3,000			
Stock		3,000	10,000	
Land			5,000	
Machinery			6,000	
D-Van			25,000	
Creditor		4,600		
A's Loan				20,000
B. Loan			5,000	
Vendor				20,000
Capital				6,000
	3,000	8,000	51,000	46,000
Net Decrease in WC	**5,000**			**5,000**

M/s Devashish Internationl Ltd., Mussoorie
Cash Flow Statement
For the year ending 31st December 201?... (Current Year)

Particular	Amount
Cash balance on 1st January, 201?... (Current Year)	**₹ 4,000**
Sources:	
From Operations (See Note 2)	₹ 45,600
Loan from Mrs. Devashish	₹ 20,000
Total Sources	₹ 69,600
Applications:	
Payment of bank loan	₹ 5,000
Payment for delivery van	₹ 5,000
Machinery acquired	₹ 15,000

Buildings acquired	₹ 5,000
Land acquired	₹ 10,000
Drawings	₹ 26,000
	₹ 66,000
Cash balance as on 31st December, 201?... (Current year)	**₹ 3,600**

(b)

M/s Devashish Internationl Ltd. Mussoorie
Funds Flow Statement
For the year ended 31st December, 201?... (Current Year)

(Amount in ₹)

Particular	Amount	Particular	Amount
Funds from Operations	41,000	Repayment of bank loan	5,000
Loan from Mrs. Devashish	20,000	Payment for delivery van	5,000
Decrease in Working Capital	5,000	Machinery acquired	15,000
		Land acquired	10,000
		Buildings acquired	5,000
		Partners' drawings	26,000
	66,000		**66,000**

Working Notes:

1.	Funds from Operations		
	Capital as on 31st December, 201?...		1,54,000
	Add: Drawing during the year		26,000
			1,80,000
	Less: Capital as on 1st January		1,48,000
			32,000
	Profit of the year		32,000
	Add: Depreciation for the year (₹ 36,000 – ₹ 27,000)		9,000
			41,000
2.	Cash from Operations:		41,000
	Add: Decrease in stock	3,000	
	Increase in creditors	4,600	7,600
			48,600
	Less: Increase in debtors		3,000
	Cash from Operations		**45,600**

Machinery Account

To Balance b/d	80,000	By Depreciation for the year	9,000
To Bank (acquired during the year)	15,000	By balance c/d	86,000
	95,000		**95,000**

Illustration 4.6

M/s JGRS Ltd. plans to expand into a new product line. In preparation, it has spent ₹ 27,50,000 in unrecoverable planning and systems work and another ₹ 22,50,000 on land and improvements, which could be sold now for ₹ 20,00,000. The future cash flows of the division were originally estimated to have a present value of ₹ 58,00,000 well worth the original ₹ 50,00,000 investment. Now, with new information, it estimates that an additional ₹ 15,00,000 must be spent and the project will be delayed six months. Estimates of returns once the new product is available have not changed.

Should the company continue the project?

What costs and returns would you compare and what considerations would you include?

Solution:

₹ 30,00,000 are spent and cannot be recovered: ₹ 27,50,000 + (₹ 22,50,000 – ₹ 20,00,000); these costs are not relevant for the NPV analysis. The relevant costs are the ₹ 15,00,000 of new spending and the ₹ 20,00,000 of recoverable value on land and improvements, for a total of ₹ 35,00,000. This is considerably less than the ₹ 58,00,000 in estimated revenue, so the project should be completed.

Illustration 4.7

M/s Surya Ltd., Mumbai is interested in assessing the cash flows associated with the replacement of an old machine by a new machine. The old machine bought a few years ago has a book value of ₹ 90,000 and it can be sold for ₹ 90,000. It has a remaining life of five years after which its salvage value is expected to be nil. It is being depreciated annually at the rate of 20 per cent (written down value method).

The new machine costs ₹ 4,00,000. It is expected to fetch ₹ 2,50,000 after five years when it will no longer be required. It will be depreciated annually at the rate of 33 1/3 per cent (written down value method). The new machine is expected to bring a saving of ₹ 1,00,000 per annum in manufacturing costs. Investment in working capital would remain unaffected. The tax rate applicable to the firm is 50 per cent.

Find out the relevant cash flow for this replacement decision. (Tax on capital gain/loss to be ignored).

Solution:

M/s Surya Ltd., Mumbai
Cash Flow

Particulars	Amount (₹)
Initial cash flow:	
Cost of new machine	4,00,000
Salvage value of old machine	90,000
	3,10,000
Subsequent annual cash flows:	

(Amount ₹ '000)

	Year 1	Year 2	Year 3	Year 4	Year 5
Savings in Costs (A)	100	100	100	100	100
Depreciation on new machine	133.3	88.9	59.3	39.5	26.3
Less: Depreciation on old machine	18.3	14.4	11.5	9.2	7.4

Therefore, incremental depreciation (B)	115.3	74.5	47.8	30.3	18.9
Net incremental saving (A – B)	–15.3	25.5	52.2	69.7	81.1
Less: Incremental Tax @ 50%	–7.6	12.8	26.1	34.8	40.6
Incremental profit	–7.7	12.7	26.1	34.9	40.5
Depreciation (added back)	115.3	74.5	47.8	30.3	18.9
Net cash flow	**107.6**	**87.2**	**73.9**	**65.2**	**59.4**

Terminal cash flow:

There will be a cash inflow of ₹ 2,50,000 at the end of 5th year when the new machine will be scrapped away. So, in the last year the total cash inflow will be ₹ 3,09,400 (*i.e.*, ₹ 2,50,000 + ₹ 59,400).

Illustration 4.8

(*a*) Write short notes on:

(*i*) Marginal cost of capital

(*ii*) Profitability Index

(*iii*) Working capital cycle.

(*b*) A company is offered a contract which has the following terms:

An immediate cash outlay of ₹ 30,000 followed by a cash inflow of ₹ 35,800 after 3 years.

What is the company's rate of return on this contract?

Solution:

(*a*) (*i*) **Marginal cost of capital:**

It is the cost of raising an additional rupee of capital. It is derived when the average cost of capital if computed with marginal weights. The weights represent the proportion of funds the firm intends to employ. The marginal cost of capital is calculated with the intended financing proportion as weights. When the funds are raised in the same proportion and if the component costs remain unchanged, there will be no difference between average cost of capital and marginal cost of capital. The component costs may remain constant upto a certain level and then start increasing. In that case both the average cost and marginal cost will increase but the marginal cost of capital will rise at a faster rate.

(*ii*) **Profitability Index:**

In capital budgeting, there are cases when we have to compare or rank a number of proposals each involving different amount of cash flows. One of the methods of comparing/ranking such proposals is to work out what is known as profitability index (PI). It is also called benefit-cost ratio. It may be calculated as follows:

$$\text{PI} = \frac{\text{Present value of net cash inflows}}{\text{Initial cash outlay}}$$

Suppose, for example a company is considering two projects *viz.*, A and B. The present value of net cash flows and initial outlay are as follows:

	Project A	Project B
	₹	₹
Present value of net cash inflows	36,000	34,000
Initial cash outlay	30,000	29,000

In the case of the above example, Project A has profitability index of 1.20 whereas Project B's ratio is 1.17 calculated as under:

$$A = \frac{₹\ 36,000}{₹\ 30,000} = 1.20$$

$$B = \frac{₹\ 34,000}{₹\ 29,000} = 1.17$$

It may be noted that as long as the profitability index is equal to or greater than 1.00, the project is acceptable.

Alternatively, profitability index may also be calculated as under

$$PI = \frac{\text{Sum of discounted cash inflows}}{\text{Sum of discounted cash outflows}}$$

(*iii*) **Working capital cycle:**

This refers to the length of time between the firm's paying cash for materials, (creditors) (entering into the production process/stock), and the inflow of cash from debtors (sales). When costs are incurred on labour, overheads and raw materials, work-in-progress (WIP) is generated.

In the production cycle, WIP is converted into finished goods. The finished goods when sold on credit, gets converted into sundry debtors. The debtors are realised after the credit period. This cash is then again used to pay for raw materials, etc. Thus there is a complete cycle from cash to cash.

Short-term funds are required to meet the requirement of money during this period. The time period is dependent upon the length of time within which the original cash gets converted into cash again. This cycle is also known as "Operating Cycle" and can be depicted as follows:

Working Capital Cycle

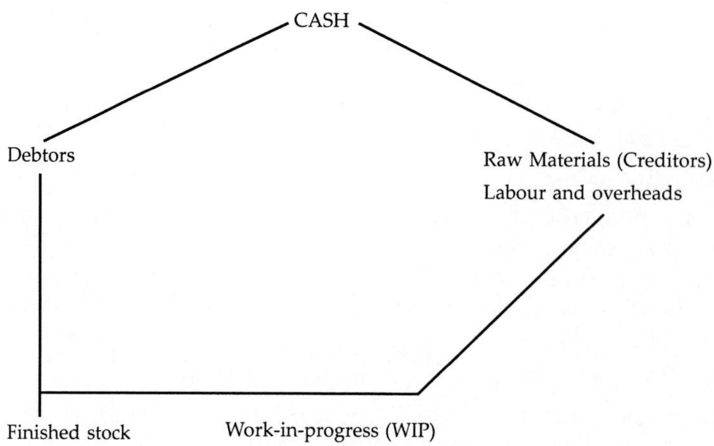

Fig. 4.1 Operating cycle

(*b*) The amount of ₹ 30,000, Cash outflow may be treated as a principal which the company deposit into an account that pays an unknown rate of interest but returns a compound amount of ₹ 35,800 after 3 years.

Now, $FV = PV (1 + r)^n$

or ₹ 35,800 = ₹ 30,000 $(1 + r)^3$

or ₹ 35,800/₹ 30,000 = $(1 + r)^3$

or $1.193 = (1 + r)^3$

In the compound value table, value closest to the value of 1.193 in the year 3 years is 6% interest rate. Thus, the actual rate of interest on the contract is slightly greater than 6%.

Illustration 4.9

M/s Madhur Limited currently has a centralised billing system. It takes around 4 days for customers mailed payments to reach the central billing location. Subsequently, it takes another $1\frac{1}{2}$ days for processing these payments, only after which deposits are made. M/s Madhur Limited has a daily average collection of ₹ 5,00,000. The company plans to initiate a lock box system in which customers mailed payments would reach the receipt location $2\frac{1}{2}$ days earlier. Further the process time would be reduced by another 1 day, since each lock box bank would mailed deposits twice daily.

You are required to:

(*i*) Determine the reduction in cash balances that can be achieved through the use of a lock box system.

(*ii*) Determine the opportunity cost of the present system, assuming a 5% return on short-term investments.

(*iii*) If the annual cost of the lock box system is ₹ 80,000, should the system be initiated?

Solution:

(*i*) Total time saving = $3\frac{1}{2}$ days

Time savings × Daily average collection = Reduction in cash balances achieved

= $3\frac{1}{2}$ × ₹ 5,00,000

= ₹ 17,50,000

(*ii*) 5% × ₹ 17,50,000 = ₹ 87,500

(*iii*) Since the opportunity cost of the present system (₹ 87,500) exceeds the cost of the lock box system (₹ 80,000), the system should be initiated.

Illustration 4.10

M/s JMS company is having difficulties with an automated grinding machine which has 4 years of service life and its operating costs are fairly sizable compared to its revenues. For the next four years, the revenues generated will be ₹ 5,20,000 annually but the annual cost expenses will be ₹ 3,80,000. In addition, it must take depreciation of ₹ 80,000 per year until the machine reaches zero book value. The machine could be sold today for net cash of ₹ 80,000 which is less than its current book value of ₹ 1,60,000. This is not good, if the machine were held for 4 years it could probably be sold for ₹ 80,000 net cash. The firm's alternative is to invest in a new grinding machine costing ₹ 4,00,000, not counting the ₹ 80,000 needed to transport and install it. The new machine would generate a revenue of ₹ 9,20,000 with cash expenses of ₹ 5,80,000. It would be depreciated over a 4 year period to a book value of ₹ 1,60,000 at which time it could be sold for ₹ 1,40,000 net cash. Depreciation would be by the straight line method. The new machine would require tying up an additional ₹ 2,00,000 of inventory and receivables over the 4 year period.

What is the differential after tax cash flow stream for this proposal?

Assume tax rate of 50% on Income and Capital gain.

Solution:

M/s JMS Ltd.

Statement showing differential after tax cash flow stream for the proposal

(Amount in ₹)

Year	New Machine	Existing Machine Cash Flow	Differential
(a)	(b)	(c)	(d) = (b) – (c)
0	-5,60,000 (Refer to working note 1)	0	-5,60,000
1	2,10,000 (Refer to working note 2)	1,10,000	1,00,000
2	2,10,000	1,10,000	1,10,000
3	2,10,000	70,000	1,40,000
4	5,60,000 (Refer to working note 3)	1,10,000	4,50,000

Working Notes:

1. **Calculation of Initial Cash Flow:**

	₹	₹
Outflow:		
Cost of New Machine	4,00,000	
Add: Transportation and installation cost of machine	80,000	4,80,000
Add: Increase in Inventory and receivables		2,00,000
Total cash outflow		6,80,000
Inflow:		
Salvage value (of old machine)	80,000	
Add: tax saving on loss 50% (₹ 1,60,000 – 80,000)	40,000	1,20,000
Net Initial outlay		**5,60,000**

2. Annual Cash Flows after tax:

	New Machine	Existing Machine	
		Year 1-2	Year 3-4
	₹	₹	₹
Annual revenues	9,20,000	5,20,000	5,20,000
Less: Cash expenses	5,80,000	3,80,000	3,80,000
Less: Depreciation (Refer to working note 3)	80,000	80,000	
Income before tax	2,60,000	60,000	1,40,000
Less: Taxes (50%)	1,30,000	30,000	70,000
Net Income after tax	1,30,000	30,000	70,000
Add: Depreciation	80,000	80,000	
Cash flow after tax	**2,10,000**	**1,10,000**	**70,000**

3. Cash Flow in the Last Year:

	New Machine	Existing Machine
	₹	₹
Book value of machine	1,60,000	
Less: Cash proceeds of machine	1,40,000	80,000
Gain/(Loss)	(20,000)	80,000
Tax Savings/(Additional Tax)	10,000	(40,000)
Add: Cash received	1,40,000	80,000
Net Cash received	1,50,000	40,000
Add: Return of working capital	2,00,000	
Add: Annual cash inflow	2,10,000	70,000
Final year cash flow	**5,60,000**	**1,10,000**

REVIEW QUESTIONS

1. (*a*) Differentiate between a Fund Flow Statement and a Cash Flow Statement.

   (*b*) What is the utility of such statements in management?

2. Which of the following should be treated as incremental cash flows?

   (*a*) A portion of existing corporate overhead.

   (*b*) Future tax benefits from the purchased business.

   (*c*) Depreciation of the new company's assets.

   A. 2

   B. 3

   C. 1, 2

   D. 1, 3

   E. 1, 2, 3

3. Which of the following should be included with cash flows?
   (*a*) The opportunity cost of resources
   (*b*) Net working capital
   (*c*) Cost of research performed before the current analysis.
   A. 1
   B. 3
   C. 1, 2
   D. 2, 3
   E. 1, 2, 3

4. Company ABC Ltd. invests ₹ 1,00,000 in a project (in year 0). It expects to receive nominal cash flows of ₹ 40,000 in year 1, ₹ 50,000 in year 2, and ₹ 60,000 in year 3, received at the end of each year. Assume inflation is projected at 5% per year and the real discount rate equals 10%.

   What is the project's net present value?

   Assume the initial investment and all cash flows occur at the end of the year.

Answers

2. A **3.** C (Statement is a sunk cost)

4. The nominal discount rate is 1.10 × 1.05 = 1.155.

The net present value of the project is – ₹ 1,00,000 + ₹ 40,000 / 1.155 + ₹ 50,000 / 1.155^2 + ₹ 60,000 / 1.155^3 = ₹ 11,053

Chapter 5

Working Capital Management

The term 'working capital' refers to a firm's investment in short-term assets, short-term securities, accounts receivables and investment. Thus, it refers to the firm's current or circulating assets. Current assets have been defined as assets that are usually converted into cash within the current accounting year. They are therefore cash or near cash resources.

The word 'working capital' originated at a time when most of the industries were closely related to agriculture. Processors used to buy the crops at the time of fall, process them and sell the products. Bank loans with a maturity period of less than a year were obtained and were paid back after the sale of the finished goods. Thus the borrowers found this capital through short-term borrowings, working very well, hence they termed it as 'working capital'.

COMPONENTS OF WORKING CAPITAL

1. Current Assets

(*i*) **Inventories or stocks:**

These are materials, commodities or the goods that the firm has at any moment of time and which are expected to be used in the production process or be sold as finished products. These include raw-materials, bought-in-components, work in progress and finished goods etc.

(*ii*) **Debtors or accounts receivable:**

These are short-term debts owed to the company created through credit sales

(*iii*) **Prepaid expenses:**

Such as unexpired insurance

(*iv*) **Short-term investment:**

Securities

(*v*) **Cash and bank balances:**

Cash in hand

Cash at Bank

2. Current Liabilities

There are short-term obligations and debts due to outside parties. 'Current' here means which is due within the current financial year. Typical items of current liabilities are:

(*i*) Creditors or Accounts Payable including Bills Payable.

(*ii*) Accrued Expenses/Expenses due

(*iii*) Bank Overdraft

(*iv*) Short-term Bank Loans, Proposed Dividend

(*v*) Tax Payment due etc.

IMPORTANCE OF WORKING CAPITAL

Technically, working capital management is an integral part of the overall financial management. It is similar to capital budgeting decision in so far as if involves an analysis of risk and profitability. However, the problems of working capital are quite dissimilar to those of capital budgeting decisions. In capital budgeting time factor is of crucial significance in its decision making whereas in case of working capital management it is not so. The most notables feature of working capital management is the striking of a balance between the conflicting issues of liquidity and profitability. More of liquidity directly affects profitability adversely and vice-versa.

However, working capital management involves managing current assets and current liabilities so as to maintain a satisfactory level of working capital. The main considerations that make working capital management so important are as follow:

1. **Large investment in current assets:**

   Current assets generally form a larger proportion of total assets. Studies made reveal the current assets are generally more than 55% of total investments. Thus they represent a large investment and have volatile nature which fact gives more importance to the management of working capital.

2. **Time devoted to working capital management:**

   In view of its impact on the total finances it is only natural that financial management has to grapple with working capital problems for most of the times. In fact fixed capital management is only episodic while working capital problems are directly linked up with the day-to-day operations and have therefore to be assigned a larger input of managerial time.

3. **Importance for small firms:**

   A small firm may minimize its investment in fixed assets by obtaining them on hire or lease basis but cannot avoid to have current assets. Moreover it may have a limited access to long-term capital market and may have to manage with short-term resources.

4. **Direct link between sales and current assets:**

   The sales growth and needs to finance current assets are very closely related. For example if your average collection period is say 30 days and sales are at a level of say ₹ 2000 per day, investment in debtors would be ₹ 60,000 and if the sales increase from ₹ 2000 to ₹ 4000 per day investment in debtors would double itself *i.e.*, ₹ 1,20,000. The Finance Manager must be vigilant on this growth.

NATURE OF WORKING CAPITAL

The circulating nature of working capital can be explained with the help of a diagram *i.e.*, Cash Cycle of the firm or Operating Cycle of the firm.

Cash Conversion Cycle

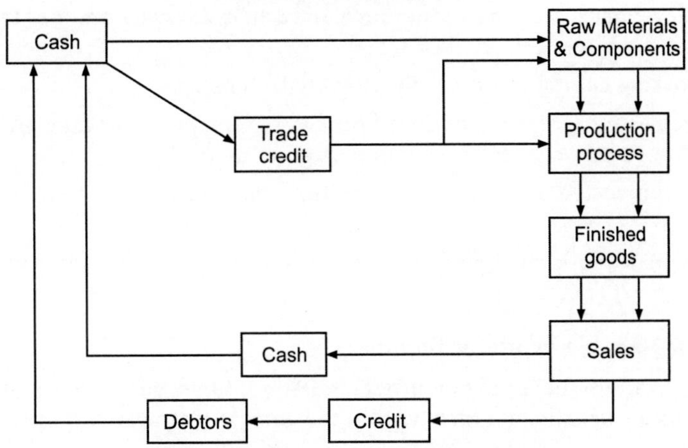

Fig. 5.1 Flow chart of cash conversion cycle

A manufacturing firm starts with cash which it invests in raw materials. Additional inventory in bought on credit creating creditors. Further trade credit and cash is used to finance production which is sold on credit creating debtors. Eventually debtors pay and cash received is used to pay creditors.

In case of retailing firm, the cycle may be very short.

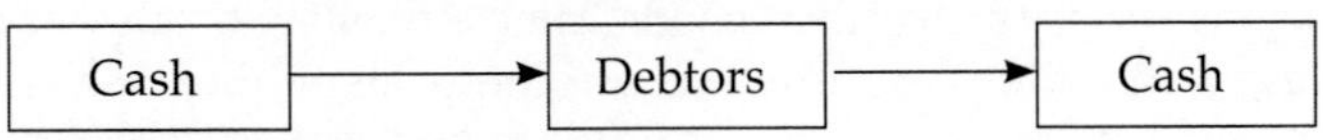

CONCEPT OF WORKING CAPITAL

There are two general working capital concepts: Gross Working Capital and Net Working Capital.

1. **Gross working capital:**

   Refers to the amount of funds invested in current assets employed in a business process. This is a going concern concept and the financial managers are more concerned with this concept since these assets are used to bring about productivity from other fixed assets.

2. **Net working capital:**

   This the difference between current assets and current liabilities. This concept is helpful to determine the short-term solvency of the firm. The creditors are more concerned with this concept.

   The Gross concept is used here since one of the most important functions of a Financial Manager is to provide the right amount of working capital at the right time in order to maximize its rate of return on its investment.

CLASSIFICATION OF WORKING CAPITAL

Broadly, working capital may be divided into two heads:

1. Permanent Working Capital
2. Temporary Working Capital or Variable Working Capital

1. Permanent Working Capital

It refers to the investment in current assets required to produce the goods and services on a continuing basis. It represents the minimum level of cash, inventories and debtors maintained by the firm to support the minimum level of sales.

Permanent working capital has the following characteristics:

(*i*) Unlike fixed assets which retain their form over a long period of time, permanent working capital is constantly changing from one asset to another.

(*ii*) The amount invested in permanent working capital may never leave business so long as it continues.

(*iii*) The permanent working capital requirements will go on increasing with the growth in sales.

2. Temporary or Variable Working Capital

This refers to the additional funds required at different times during the year. Like permanent working capital this also change its form within the current financial period.

DETERMINANTS OF WORKING CAPITAL

Some of factors that affect the need of working capital are:

1. **Nature of business:**

   Working capital requirements are directly dependent on the nature of business. A manufacturing-cum-marketing (distributing) firm may require more of working capital. Public utilizes like telephone, electricity, water, supply etc. may required less of working capital as they are selling service rather than goods. They are selling on almost cash basis. Empirical studies reveal that the proportion of current assets to total assets in case of tobacco, construction and trading firms is 80% to 90%, in case of electricity, water supply, telephone, etc. is 20–30% and low in case of hotels, restaurants etc. is 10–20%.

2. **Period of manufacture of production cycle:**

   If the period of manufacture is very large, the working capital requirements will be more. A distillery company engaged in selling 100 years old wine, will have a large amount of working capital invested in inventories as compared to a bakery manufacturing and selling cakes or biscuits everyday.

3. **Terms of purchase and sale:**

   A firm buying on cash and selling on credit will require large amounts of working capital as compared to a firm buying on credit and selling on cash. If the firm receives orders and advance payments against orders like heavy machine building, the working capital requirements will be lower.

4. **Trade cycles:**

   Business ups and downs *i.e.,* fluctuations are termed as crade cycles. There are four phases of a trade cycle *i.e.,* (*a*) Boom (*b*) Recession

(*c*) Depression, and (*d*) Recovery.

Boom phase is characterised with rising prices and overall growth and prosperity in business activity. During this phase working capital requirements are likely to be larger than in depression phase when business activity declines to low-levels. (Ref. Fig. 5.2)

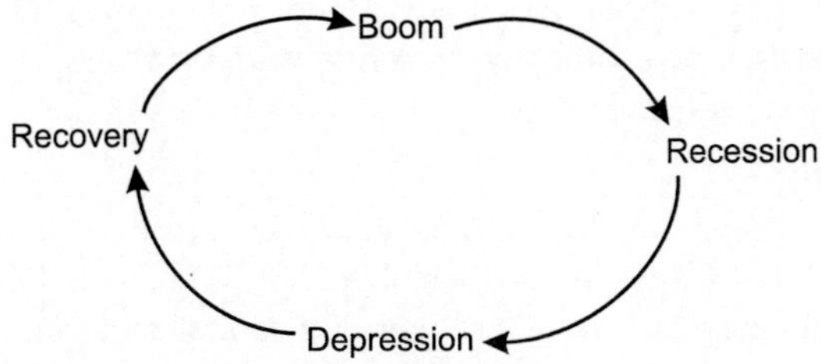

Fig. 5.2 Trade cycle

5. **Seasional nature and production policy:**

   Certain products are required only at a particular seasonals like woolen garments, ice-cream, Rakhis for Raksha Bandhan etc. These firm has to produce throughout the year to building up enough of inventory-reserves. They would require larger amounts of working capital.

6. **Credit Policy:**

   A firm following a liberal trade credit policy will have higher amounts tied up in debtors. Consequently higher amount of working capital.

7. **Growth and expansion:**

   As a company grows it is only natural that it would require more of working capital. However the working capital requirements precede the growth rather than following it.

8. **Degree of machanisation:**

   Working capital requirements directly depend on degree of machanisation. A fully mechanized plant in capital intensive industries will require less of working capital as compared to labour intensive industries.

9. **Availability of raw-materials:**

   If raw material availability is continuous a smaller amount of working capital may be sufficient as compared to a situation when supply of raw material is irregular, uncertain, and seasonal. In the letter case more working capital will be needed.

10. **Profit level:**

    Retained earnings form an important source of financing working capital requirements. If a company has high profit-levels which bring day-to-day cash, it helps in the coordination between different activities.

11. **Coordination:**

    An efficient management has perfect coordination between production and sales so that things needed are produced in time. Further, when a company is operating on a national or international level, a complete coordination between inflow or out-flow at various centers of operation will minimize the requirements of working capital.

12. **Managements attitude towards risk:**

    Risk averting management will like to keep more of working capital available to it as compared to risk taking management who may like to operate at a lower level of working capital. Working capital requirements may be lower if the management is risk-taking.

13. **Divident policy:**

    A company following a liberal cash dividend policy may require more of working capital as dividends, cause outflow of funds and vice-versa, *i.e.*, less working capital with conservature dividend policy.

14. **Depreciation policy:**

    Depreciation allows generated funds to be retained in business. If a company charges higher depreciation it will leave amount as divisible profits. The tax liability will be low as well as dividend payments may be low. Hence working capital requirements may be lower.

15. **Access to the capital market:**

    If a firm has an easy access to source of finance, it may operate at a lower level of working capital and in times of needs it may immediately obtain funds.

Determining working capital requirements needs a balancing of many factors together and that is why it is a fairly complex task.

THEORY OF WORKING CAPITAL

Working capital is employed only when actual production is undertaken and the volume required is generally determined by the level of production. The precise level of investment in working capital depends on:

1. Management's attitude towards risk. Risk in this context refers to the risk of not maintaining sufficient current assets to:
    (*i*) Meet all short-term obligations as they mature, and
    (*ii*) Support the proper level of sales.
2. Factors that affect the amount of cash, inventories, accounts receivables and other current assets as discussed above.

Walker suggests four principles that form the basis for a theory of working capital:

1. If working capital is varied relative to sales, the amount of risk that a firm assumes is also varied and the opportunity for gain or loss is increased.

    The principle implies that there exists a definite relation between risk and rate of return *i.e.*, when the level of working capital relative to sales decreases (the risk increases) the opportunity for gain from investment increases and vice-versa. Gains can be measured but losses can't be measured. The principles suggest that the management should choose a level of working capital that maximizes the rate of return. Further a conservative management would employ more working capital for a given volume of sales than one which is aggressive and is ready to assume greater risks.
2. Capital should be invested in each component of working **capital,** as long as the equity position of the firm increases.
3. Type of capital used to finance current assets: The type of capital used for finance to current assets directly affects the amounts of risk that a firm assume as well as the opportunity for gain or loss and the cost of capital.

A firm trying to minimize risk will employ only equity but in so doing it will force the opportunity of higher return on equity (due to trading on equity) (*Ref. Chapter 2 Long-term Finance and Capital Structure*).

4. Nature of contracts negotiated by borrowers: The financial manager is concerned with the restrictive clauses contained in these contracts and the maturity dates of these contracts. The ability to pay short-term obligations directly depends upon the cash inflow rather than earnings. Thus greater the disparity between the maturity of a firm's short-term debt instruments and inflow of internally generated funds, the greater the risk and vice-versa.

RECEIVABLES MANAGEMENT

Accounts Receivables or debtors represent sales that are made on credit. The level of accounts receivables are a function of:

1. Level of sales
2. The credit terms
3. The riskiness of individual customers and seasonal influence.
4. The managements attitude towards risk.

By making influence more attractive a firm can increase its sales turnover, however, granting credit also involves costs of finance tied up in accounts receivables, increased administrative expenses, and probabilities of bad debts occurring.

The management of accounts receivable is therefore primarily concerned with trade off between the profits from increase sales generated by credit policies and the cost of such policies although competitive pressure acts as a major constraint, management still have enough scope within which to formulate receivables policies.

The objective of any accounts receivables policy should be to maximise profits. This will mean that the policy established should be one, which optimises accounts receivables, inventory and cash as a whole, for example the liabilities structure of the company may require a certain cash balance profile to be kept. Additionally the cost of holding stocks may be so great (*e.g.*, storage) that it may be optimum to increase the credit terms to induce advanced sales, *e.g.*, in the cases where the cost of financing debt is less than the storage cost of inventory. As a general rule the firm should expand credit facilities so long as the profitability of sales generated exceeds the increased cost of accounts receivables.

FUNCTION OF ACCOUNT RECEIVABLE MANAGEMENT

The main functions of accounts receivable management are:

1. The cash discount quantum and period
2. The credit period
3. The customers to accept for credit sales
4. The collection policy.

Cash discount directly affects a firm's cost of capital, similarly credit period and cash discount period have same effect and considerations. The aim of the credit assessment is to determine the probable bad debts. Deliquent accounts have the same effect on the net worth as the cost of capital, cash discount or the credit terms. Tools are bank reference, trade reference. In order to avoid the losses of bad debts, the management may eliminate that customer or charge him higher rates (if price differenciation is possible), where probability of bad debt is more.

INVENTORY MANAGEMENT

Inventories comprise of raw-materials, goods in process and finished goods. The objective of holding inventory are, avoiding losses of sales, gaining quantity discounts, achieving efficient production and reducing ordering costs. However, the inventory holding costs of a firm includes:

1. Material costs
2. Order cost
3. Carrying cost-storage, insurance, obsolescence, damage or theft
4. Cost of funds tied up in inventory
5. Cost of running out of goods.

Effective management of inventory involves a trade off between having too much inventory and too little inventory, keeping in view the above advantages and cost involved.

A system of effective inventory management involves three sub systems:

1. Economic order quantity
2. Recorder point
3. Stock level.

The finance manager's and the accountant's role in inventory management will almost certainly help in planning the management information system and a stock/recording procedures.

CASH MANAGEMENT

Cash forms the method of collecting revenues and paying various costs and expenses for business. The reasons for holding cash have traditionally been divided into three categories as postulated by Keynes:

1. The transaction motive
2. The precautionary motive, and
3. The speculative motive.

The transaction motive is the need for the cash to meet the payment arising in the normal course of day-to-day business. A balance of cash is kept essentially to synchronise the receipt and payments of a business.

Yet another motive to hold cash is called compensation motive, *i.e.*, cash to be maintained with bankers in order to become their important customers. Similarly, indirectly compensating them for their service. Further banks require a minimum balance to be kept in the account.

The precautionary motive for holding cash relates to the need for creating readily available funds to meet unexpected circumstances, the more uncertain the cash flows are, the greater the precautionary balance that have to be kept. A company having a very good access to short-term borrowing may have lesser amount of precautionary balance. The speculative motive relates to holding cash so that resources are available with which to take advantage of profitable opportunities. In general, a business firm should not speculate with cash balance, this being true, no further attention is given to this aspect of holding cash.

OBJECTIVES

The main objective in managing cash is to trade off between liquidity and profitability in order to maximise long-run profits. By keeping greater amount of cash (liquidity) the firm is able to meet its debt comfortably and the creditor confidence is kept and the risk of technical insolvency reduced. However, current account cash does not earn any interest and so the greater the amount or resources left as cash balances, the less the profit earning potential of the firm, in extreme cases this lack of profitability will result in shareholder's dissatisfaction and takeover. If cash balance is reduced to nil short-term profitability increases as recourses are invested in revenue earning assets, in the longer-term, however, the damage to credit impairment caused by shortage of liquidity will almost certainly lead to reduced profits. Thus, management has to develop a policy of striking a balance between the two.

Factors Influencing Cash Balances

The amount of cash needed for transaction purposes is predictable and depends mainly upon two factors:

1. The credit position of the firm
2. Status of firm's receivables.

With a view to control cash flows, cash budget is prepared. Cash budget is simply a cash flow forecast. It is a technique to predict the amount of funds and the time when these funds would be required by the organization. It is a brief summary of projected cash-in-flows and cash out-flows. It requires making an estimates of future cash flows. Such a budget reveals cash surplus or deficiency which the management must look into. The management must invest idle funds and arrange for borrowings in case of shortfall.

Management of Cash Balances

Management of cash balances involves a two-pronged attack *i.e.,* accelerating the cash inflows and delaying cash outflows. Accelerating cash inflows needs minimizing the time-lag between when the payment is made by our client and when it is received at our end. The various techniques are

1. **Lock box system:**

   The company creates postal boxes located near the main customers who are requested to send payments direct to postal box. The company's bank operate these boxes and give credit to the company immediately once the cheques or drafts are locally cleared.

2. **Concentrated banking centers:**

   Another technique used is creation of collection centers at different places. The cheques, so collected, are cleared and money credited to the company by wire (TT).

3. **Special handling of payment:**

   The disbursement of cash should be controlled remembering that any technique to delay the payment beyond the due date is bad and should be avoided. Generally, firms adopt a method of centralized payment *i.e.,* all payments are to be made by head office where all branches and factories are supposed to send the purchase invoices for payment.

Management of Working Capital

Inspite of a lot of academic exercises done by a number of intellectuals in the field of finance, the working capital management has not been optimised. It is because there are various functional areas having conflicting demands. For example, production department needs more of raw material to avoid stoppage in production process. The marketing manager needs high levels of finished goods to avoid loss of sales, high incentives, larger days of credit, etc. Each of these require funds involving huge costs of which managers are not aware. Hence there is a need for a central agency to plan and control working capital.

Financial Working Capital Requirements

There are various sources of finance available to be a company but before a decision is reached as to the type of securities to be used for financing working capital, it would be appropriate to look into the nature of working capital needs. As discussed earlier the working capital may be either permanent or temporary. Permanent working capital refers to the minimum of each component of working capital needs to support sales at a particular level. Such needs are permanent and funds tied up in these components are not likely to be released so long as company is functioning. Such requirements must be furnished from long-term sources such as equity, preference, retained earnings and long-term loans. As regards temporary working capital needs these can be financed from short-term sources such as bank loans, bank overdraft, trade credit and other short term borrowings.

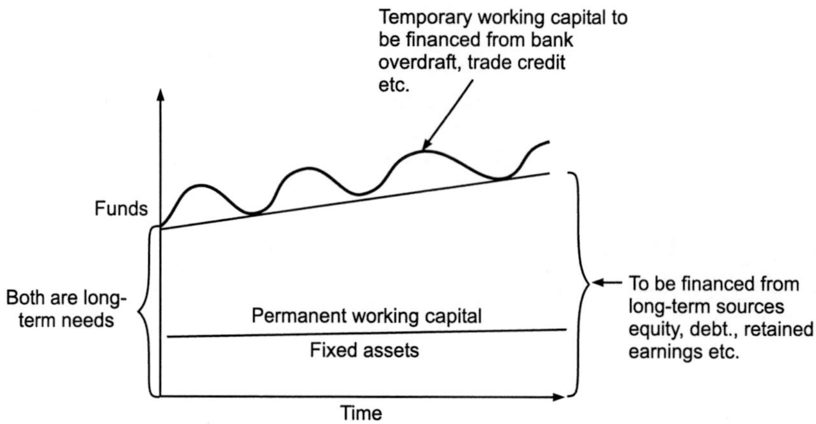

Fig. 5.3 How to finance working capital

The Tandon Committee Report

In July, 1974, the Reserve Bank of India constituted a study group under the chairmanship of Shri P.L. Tandon to suggest guidelines for the rational allocation and optimum use of credit form the banks. Bank credit, being a scarce source, has to be optimally used. Before the setting up of the committee, the lending practice by banks was to give 75 per cent of the value of inventory and receivables. This inventory included even inventory purchased from creditors who where not yet paid. Hence it was double financing. The terms of reference of the Committee were:

1. What continues the working capital requirements of industry?
2. What is the end use of credit?
3. Can lending style be improved?

The Tandon Committee's recommendations are based on the following points:

The entire working capital needs of firms cannot be financed by bankers alone. The banker should finance only a part of it and the rest should be financed by the firm itself. The Committee popularized the concept of working capital gap.

The committee suggested three stages of ascertaining permissible level of bank-borrowings.

1st Stage:

25 per cent of the working capital gap be financed by the firm from long-term sources:

Suppose total current assets	₹ 400 lakh
Suppose current liabilities (other than bank borrowings)	₹ 160 lakh
Working capital gap	₹ 240 lakh
25% to be financed by the firm	₹ 60 lakh
Bank borrowing	₹ 180 lakh

This means that bank borrowings would be maximum of 75 per cent of working capital gap.

2nd Stage:

The committee recommended that the borrower would finance 25% of total Current Assets from long-term sources:

	(₹ in Lakhs)
Total current assets	400
25% to be financed by firm	100
	300
Less current liabilities	160
Maximum bank borrowings permissible	₹ 140 lakhs

3rd Stage or Ideal Method of Borrowing Limit:

The committee recommended that every firm has some core assets which must be carried by a firm at all times lest the production comes to a halt.

Suppose current assets needed	₹ 400 lakh
Further suppose core assets are	90 lakh
Other current assets	310 lakh
25% of other current assets to be financed by firm	78 lakh
	232 lakh
Less current liabilities	160 lakh
Maximum bank borrowing permissible	**₹ 72 lakh**

The committee viewed the role of a banker to supplement the borrower's resources in carrying a reasonable level of current assets in relation to the production requirements.

Again a Core Panel was set up to review the implementation of Tandon Committee recommendations. This panel recommended to reduce the dependence of companies on commercial banks for their working capital requirements. Its major recommendation was that borrowers should enhance their contribution to working capital. It was suggested that companies be placed in 2nd stage as recommended by Tandon Panel. This would give a minimum current ratio of 1.33 to 1. The committee further recommended that this should be made compulsory for all units having working capital limits of ₹ 100 lakh or more.

Excess borrowings are to be segregated and made repayable within 5 years.

The Core report further observed that segregation of core assets under ideal method 3rd of Tandon Panel was not practicable.

The Core committee stressed the need to make a detailed study to establish the relationship between prices, production and credit.

Illustration 5.1

M/s Modern Tech Corporation, Chandigarh sells goods in the domestic market at a gross profit of 25 per cent (not counting depreciation as part of cost of goods sold). Its figures for one year of operations are given below:

M/s Modern Tech Corporation, Chandigrah

	Particular	Amount in ₹
1.	Sales in the domestic market at one month credit	12,00,000
2.	Sales in foreign market at three month's credit (Sale price 10% below domestic market)	5,40,000
3.	Material used (suppliers extending two months credit)	4,50,000
4.	Wages paid, half month in arrears	3,60,000
5.	Manufacturing expenses paid, one month in arrear	5,40,000
6.	Administrative expenses paid, one month in arrear	1,20,000
7.	Sales promotion expenses paid, quarterly in advance	60,000
8.	Income tax payable in four installments, one of which falls in the next year	1,50,000

The company keeps one month's stock to each of raw materials and finished goods and believes in keeping ₹ 1,00,000 available to it including an overdraft limit of ₹ 50,000 not yet utilised. Assume a safety margin of 15% ascertain working capital requirements. There was no work-in-progress.

Find out the working capital needed by the company.

Solution:

Calculation of Current Assets to be Maintained in Terms of Cash Cost

(Amount in ₹)

S.No.	Particulars	Detail	
1.	**Debtors**		
	(*i*) **Home Market**		
	12,00,000 sales at 25% profit		
	Hence cost of sales	= (12,00,000 – 3,00,000) = 9,00,000	
	One month credit	$= \frac{9,00,000}{12} =$	75,000

(*ii*) **Export Market**

Selling price = 90 as it is 10% below Home Market the cost as ascertained above ₹ 75,000. Hence, 15/90 is the element of profit.

Therefore, $\frac{5,64,000 \times 15}{90}$ = ₹ 90,000

5,40,000 – 90,000 = 4,50,000

	$= \frac{4,50,000 \times 3}{12}$		1,12,500
2.	Prepaid Sales Promotion Expenses	$= \frac{60,000}{4}$	15,000
3.	Stock of Raw Material	$= \frac{4,50,000}{12}$	37,500
4.	Stock of Finished Goods	$\frac{1}{12}$ (9,00,000 + 4,50,000) =	1,12,500
5.	Cash at Bank		50,000
	Total Current Assets (C.A.)		**4,02,500**
	Less Current Liabilities		
	Creditors for Goods = $\frac{4,50,000}{6}$	= 75,000	
	Wages Outstanding = $\frac{3,60,000}{24}$	= 15,000	
	Manufacturing Expenses = $\frac{5,40,000}{12}$	= 45,000	
	Administrative Expenses = $\frac{1,20,000}{12}$	= 10,000	
	Tax Liability = $\frac{1,50,000}{4}$	= 37,500	1,82,500
6.	Net working capital		2,20,000
	Add 15% Margin		33,000
7.	**Working capital needed**		**₹ 2,53,000**

CAPITAL BUDGETING—CAPITAL EXPENDITURE DECISION

Capital budgeting encompasses the generation of investment proposals, estimation of their each flows and risk associated with each project, evaluation of these cash inflows, the selection of projects based on an acceptance criteria and finally continuous revaluation of investment projects after their acceptance.

Capital budgeting involves the entire process of planning expenditures, the returns of which are expected to extend beyond one year. The use of one year as a line of demarcation is somewhat arbitrary but it is a convenient out off period. It suggests that investment in any asset with a life of less than a year fails in the realism of working capital management whereas any asset budgeting, for example purchase of fixed assets like plant building, machinery etc.

Capital budgeting decision may be defined as the firm's decision to invest its current funds most efficiently in long-term activities in anticipation of an expected flow of future benefits over a series of years. These future benefits may be in the form of increased revenues or reduction in costs or both. Thus capital budgeting may involve:

1. Replacement
2. Expansion
3. Modernisation
4. Diversification
5. Strategic investment proposals, and
6. Research and development etc.

Features of Capital Budgeting

1. Current funds exchanged for future benefits.
2. Investment of funds in long-term activities.
3. Potentially large anticipated benefits. These may occur over a long series of years.
4. Relatively high degree of risk.
5. A wide time gap between current expenditure and returns in terms of future inflows.

Overview of Capital Budgeting

In order to maximise shareholders wealth through market value of shares following are some of the measures:

1. Project Generation

Investment proposals of various types may originate at different levels within the firm, these may be:

(*i*) Adding new product line
(*ii*) Expansion of capacity
(*iii*) Cost reduction measures.

2. Project Evaluation

Involves

(*i*) Estimation of benefits and costs to be measured in terms of cash flows.
(*ii*) Selection of an appropriate criterion to judge the desirability of the project.
(*iii*) Ascertainment of:
 (*a*) cash inflows, and
 (*b*) risk involved is rather a difficult job for which experts are needed.

3. Project Selection

Screening and selection procedure may differ from firm to firm but the top management must take due care in selecting projects.

4. Project Execution

Sufficient funds should be raised or appropriated. A comprehensive capital budget is prepared *i.e.,* a formal plan for funds allocation be prepared for executive execution.

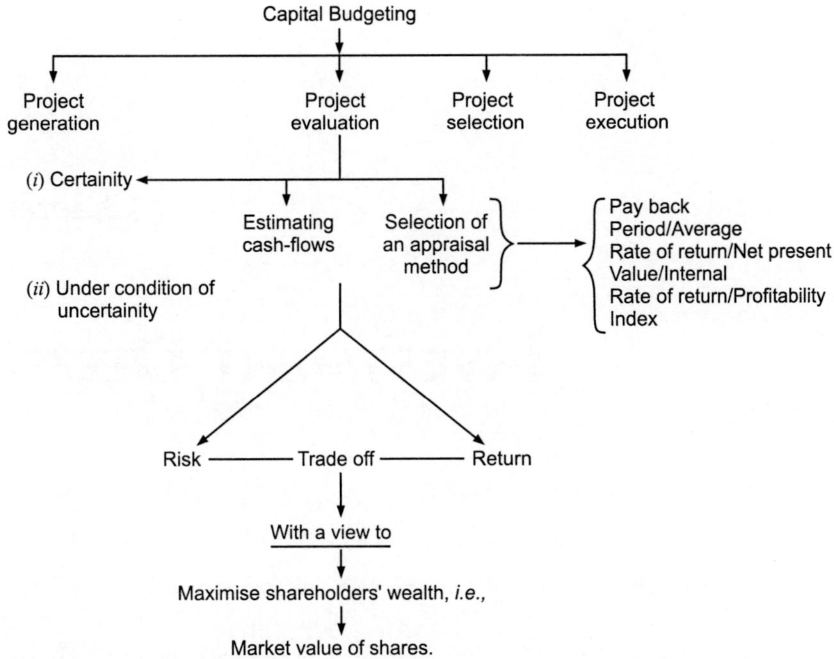

Fig. 5.4 An overview of capital budgeting

Special Features of Capital Budgeting

1. Capital budgeting involves huge amount.
2. These decisions have a long-term implication and influence the risk complexion of the firm.
3. Such decisions are irreversible decisions.
4. These decisions affect the company's future cost structure and thus determine its profit earning capacity and profitability.
5. Capital budgeting decision determines firm's ability to complete in the market place.

REVIEW QUESTIONS

1. Explain the following methods of project evaluation:
   (*a*) Payback period,
   (*b*) Accounting rate of return,
   (*c*) Net present value methods.

2. Explain the nature and significance of working capital.

3. Write a detailed note on:
   (*a*) Cash management, (*b*) Receivables,
   (*c*) Management and (*d*) Inventory management.

4. What do you understand by capital budgeting?

5. Why decisions are considered important?

Chapter 6

Investment Decisions

One of the most important, characteristic of investment in any industry is the considerable amount of capital involved. This is the principal factor in any examination of the financial feasibility of a project, subsequent to completion of the market feasibility study. Decisions about the capitalization of the project are absolutely critical to its survival. Examples of over-capitalisation in a project indicate that this is by no means a simple proposition though it is very much at the heart of project planning. There are too many instances where, given the capital cost, the physical design of the facilities, and the prevailing market conditions, the project cannot be viable, however expert or skilful the management responsible for their operation. The project investment may be divided into two parts:

1. *Exterior assets*
   (*a*) Land
   (*b*) Buildings and
   (*c*) Fixed plant.
2. *Interior assets*
   (*a*) Furniture
   (*b*) Fittings
   (*c*) Operating equipment and working capital.

Both these type of investments are substantial. They act as the natural basis for a splitting of the risk in many project ventures and this has a number of implications. At a given level of the market, the revenue potential is fixed. Thus the way in which this is divided between the parties involved in the project is crucial to the profitability of their respective investments. Usually the developer — who might represent a finance company, insurance company or bank—is looking for a low risk situation. The purchase of exterior assets provides such a situation. If the project fails exterior assets may be sold to cover the initial investment. The exterior be leased or rented to the second party, the operator. The operator's investment in interior assets is much lower, perhaps only one-fifth that of the developers, but the risk is much higher and interior assets tend to have low resale value. For all practical purposes it is seen that in very few cases is the entire investment carried by one organization. This is not to say that many existing properties are not owned freehold by the company operating them. For all new projects the investment is split is some way and the first concern of the operator is to examine the way in which the risk is shared.

Some industries has a high fixed cost type of business. Whether it is full or empty certain charges have to be met. Heat, light, power and maintenance have to be paid, along with some of the staff; most substantial of all, capital charges such as rent, interest or leasing costs, are still incurred.

Few business operate in totally stable conditions. When they first open, it often takes two or three years to build up business to a satisfactory level. Even then, throughout the year, the level of business may vary according to the season. If the developer insists on a high fixed rent or level of interest, this may mean no operating profits in the first few years and a highly volatile profit situation thereafter. Thus the implications are of three types:

1. Capital Contribution
2. Capital Charges
3. Revenue.

1. Capital Contribution

The capitalisation of the project must be as low as possible, preferably in consistent with the needs of the market. It often involves trading off capital versus operating costs. For example, the use of low quality materials in the construction may cheapen the capital cost but may result in higher operating costs, as maintenance would have to be carried out more frequently. The capitalisation and design tend to lock the operator into a certain level of operating costs which is difficult to change. Thus an in-expensive or poorly designed property operation may be very labour intensive to operate. For this reason, we find older properties are often more expensive to operate than new ones, since they were built in a different cost environment (labour was cheap).

2. Capital Charges

These may be represented in the form of rent, interest or leasing costs. They are obviously linked to the level of capitalisation. In general, the greater the instability of the project the greater the need to share the risk. This means that rents should comprise both a fixed and a variable portion, the latter varying in relation to some element of the business such as revenue.

3. Revenue

These are inextricably linked with the other two. An up market business is going to require more investment to support its image. It will incur more capital charges but must correspondingly be able to generate more revenue. In order to get this balance right, the market feasibility study must aim to identify as accurately as possible the potential value of each market segment and the marketing mix most likely to exploit that potential successfully.

THE INVESTMENT AND THE MARKET

All entrepreneurs must intent on the minimization of risk and the maximization of return. Within this range there are a number of possibilities. It is in the identification of these factors and the manner in which they are correctly related to one another, that the success of an investment analysis lies. This success can only be measured when the planned return is, or is not, eventually realised. Thus decisions taken in connection with the market and the investment have a very long time span. It may be several years before they can be evaluated. The outcome depends on two things.

(*a*) The data, and

(*b*) The way in which the data are processed.

The completeness of the data, the need for a precise identification of all relevant factors, need is be stressed. The way in which the data are processed, the manner in which they are cross-related, links very closely to the methods chosen. First, however, it is apparent that before the worth of an investment can be established, a clear policy based on the examination of the market must be produced.

The principal purpose of policy is to serve as a statement of intentions, and in this context it is concerned with a precise definition of the type of project to be provided. This will naturally include all the details relating to the recommended marketing mix. Policy will act as a basis for the examination of the investment. Revenue, operating costs and the preliminary estimate of the capital cost of the project will all be based on policy.

Once the feasibility and the desirability of the investment is established it is this same policy which will be expanded to form any brief for the detailed planning of the project and act as the guide for the accomplishment of operational objectives.

The emergent policy based on the examination of the market and the recommended marketing mix provides the starting point in the appraisal of the investment. Considerations arising from this appraisal may require modification of the policy with in constraints imposed by the market. For instance, price is an element of the marketing mix to which recommendations would be attached. The recommendations would have been arrived at using criteria which relate to the entire spectrum of the conceptual model of the market. The recommended level of pricing would have been aimed at maximising the volume of sales for a given strategy. However, this level of pricing may prove inconsistent with the level if costs associated with the product from an investment standpoint? The margin which may exist for adjusting price upwards without alienating the market will need to be assessed. Alternatively the marketing mix might be changed through a reduction in the cost of its component parts. Such economies in the recommended mix might result in alienation of the market. It is in reconciling needs of the market with the realities of the investment that the final policy must be shaped.

The essential of an approach committed to the marketing concept is that any investment must be made within the framework of the needs of the market. Many contemporary approaches begin with requirements of the investment, which act as the sole determinants for the product, and the price at which it is to be offered. It is evident that such approaches which ignore the market, in all but an intuitive manner, are hazardous, and a lower probability may be attached to their chances of success. For examples—the potential return on investment is always that which that circumstances of the market, in fulfilling its needs, will support. There may be vastly differing returns on investment even from similar projects in the same industry. The minimisation of costs, both capital and operating, without detriment to the relationship between the product and market is obviously vital in determining the extent to which an investment eventually succeeds. The right approach must be both market and cost oriented because it is in the delicate balance achieved between these two consideration that the significant investment evaluation takes place.

Policy, itemising all details of the marketing mix and its associated strategies, must be related to the period of time for which the investment is to be evaluated. The volume of business and the operating costs must obviously be forecast for that same period of time. The capital cost of the project must be accurately estimated, as must the cost of servicing that capital. The problem is to supply these detailed and necessarily accurate data for a building and business not yet in existence other than in the form of descriptions in a policy statement. This is one of the principal difficulties to be resolved in examining the investment.

GENERAL ECONOMIC CONDITIONS

Inflation and government economic policy are hardly predictable for as little as two to three years ahead. These factors are bound up with the politics of the day and even the most astute political commentator has difficulty in anticipating the intentions of the government in office. The importance of this problem to the entrepreneur is illustrated by the fact that some very large companies now appoint a political adviser in order to predict future actions.

There are some highly developed countries where the government does not prepare and publish economic plans for some future period such as five or ten years. In these countries, this is one aspect of an economic climate that has resulted in a growing uncertainty and lack of confidence on the part of investors. Combined with other factors such as the heavy dependence of the economy on imported raw materials and food, an industrial structure which clings to low technology manufactures, and a party political system, economic policy has resulted in a relative decline in positive.

Now the increasing power and availability of computers, has led to an improvement in the sophistication of econometric models which aim to plot the course of the economy and a number of agencies regularly issue predictions about likely conditions in the short and medium-term. The economy of these countries is particularly responsive to international trading conditions and of course to the decisions made in the influential economies of the developed nations. It may hard also be useful to obtain forecasts from overseas observers of the international scene.

One aspect of the decline of the economics position of these nations is the weakening currencies—has been very good for some sectors of the economy. Continued worldwide over-capacity in air transport has led to fierce competition and a reduction of air fares in real terms on most major routes.

Another aspect of this decline, a weakening currency in a country with a high dependence on imports, is associated with a rate of inflation which would have been considered very high a decade or so ago. Along with a number of unpleasant side effects, inflation can work to the long-term benefit of a high fixed-cost investment. In money terms, an inflationary environment tends to mean that, as time goes by, revenues increase. Now it is probable that at least a part of the capital charges of a business will be fixed. Inflation tends to ensure that even highly capitalised projects will move into profitability in the medium to long-term (say five to fifteen years).

This outcome is not enough to justify the project. Large net cash outflows in the early years of a project are enough to bring a company to bankruptcy is some cases. The future value of money is not equivalent to its present value. If we were able to invest ₹ 900 today at an interest rate of 10 per cent, then in a year we should have ₹ 1,000. Turned around, we could say that ₹ 1,000 to be received one year hence is equivalent to only ₹ 900 received today. Under these conditions, money earned in the early life of an investment is worth more than that in later year and future profits have to be converted to their present equivalent before they can be fully assessed. This is true quite apart from the factor of inflation, which means that future rupees will also buy less as well.

FINANCING AND OPERATING THE INVESTMENT

The method of financing a project limits the sources of capital that might be available and also the degree of risk involved. Where borrowed capital is employed or where assets are hired or leased, sufficient profits must be generated on a continuous basis to ensure that capital charges can be met. Such considerations influence the appraisal of the investment and this may be approached in two ways:

1. To what extent is the investment feasible if using a certain method of financing?

Or

2. What method of financing is required to provide a feasible investment?

The extent to which methods of financing exist for any one project depends on the parties and the particular set of circumstances involved. When assets are hired or leased it is not unusual for the lessee to seek reduced payments for the first two or three years of operation. The volume of sales will only rise gradually and then level off for a further extended period. In this situation, the lessor may insist on the provision of financial guarantees, and on evidence of proven managerial competence in the field.

One of the aspects of discussing the return on investment in a new project, is that it is usually considered only from the point of view of the interested party, that is, the operator. In fact, his investment may only be a portion of the total investment. Where there is much hiring or leasing of assets and where a high proportion of borrowed capital is concerned, there may be a number of parties participating in the same investment. The rate of return which each party anticipates will, more or less, be related to the share of risk which each undertakes. The feasibility of the investment as a whole, within the agreed financial structure, is of importance to each of the parties. The ability of the one party to operate the project profitably influences, in turn, the ability of each of the other parties to achieve with certainty the desired returns on their respective investments. Whether the structure of the operating party's organization is that of a sole proprietorship, partnership or limited company, these comments remain true.

It must be recognised that the financial return is a remuneration for both an intangible investment, knowledge, and a tangible investment, money, and for the relative risk undertaken. This concept is especially important to grasp when an increasing number of companies are receiving substantial profits for undertaking risk and investing knowledge while barely being involved in the investment of capital. A company which is the lessee of all the assets of a project, both building and equipment, may be committing almost no capital. It is committing its human resources, however, and it is risking the possibility of losses. Should it make a profit, the accountant's traditional ways of relating this to capital invested are not relevant. It should be related more appropriately to the knowledge and management skill invested. The real investment is in top supervisory people together with that portion of time required to be given by central office personnel. If this investment in one place results in only a small return or even a loss, then expressing this in actual financial terms may be misleading. What one has to consider is how much greater the return might have been if these same resources of knowledge had been invested elsewhere?

In cases where assets are leased, the entrepreneur who has invested the actual capital in the construction and equipping of the project be disregarded. As the lessor, he is accepting a large portion of the risk and has sought to assure himself of a reduced but satisfactory return measured in conventional terms.

In investment appraisal method, the investment is only expressed in terms of capital outlay. The outcome of the exercise must, however, be weighed against an assessment of the intangible investment according to circumstances.

PREPARING A DRAFT POLICY

Critical Areas of Investment Decisions

There are six areas which provide the 'conceptual framework' of the investment. The flow chart and the sequence in which the areas may imply a rigidity of approach that is not intended. No sharp delineation exists between areas, the preparation and processing of information is dynamic and may vary from one project to another. (Ref. Fig. 6.1)

There six critical are as are:

1. The draft policy
2. Forecast of gross operating profits
3. Method of financing
4. Life of the investment
5. Investment appraisal
6. The final decision.

The starting point for the draft policy must be to take a fixed volume of business to be expected. The market feasibility study will provide a forecast of likely volumes of business and this may be refined, by a preliminary decision on pricing. Both price and volume decisions will be modified many times as the project progresses but it is important to the development of policy that it is always written in the context of a certain volume and revenue.

Investment Decision

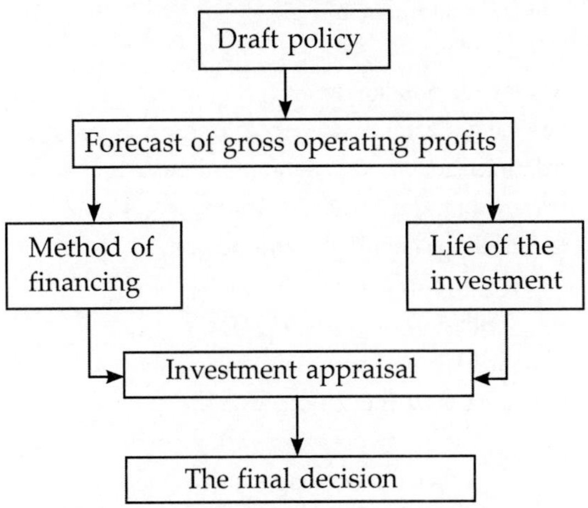

Fig. 6.1 Critical areas of investment decision

The draft policy is a necessary prerequisite of any detailed consideration of the investment.

It follows from the study of the market and it expands on the recommended marketing mix in such a way that the project in its entirely is thoroughly sketched out from a policy and a procedural standpoint. When reconciled with the requirements of the investment it can be developed as the basis for the final design. The draft policy must eventually stand against both capital and operating cost-estimates. Finally it must act as the basis of the actual product offered. Policy is the vital connecting link between the market and the investment. The policy, gradually develops and refines. It also acts as the same vital link at every stage of the process of project planning.

The draft policy be developed in consultation with the specialists who will eventually be concerned with the detailed design. Its conclusion is a statement of feasibility and a justification for continuance of the project. Such a statement cannot be made without accurate cost estimates. Any appraisal of the investment not based on accurate cost estimates would be worthless. How detailed an outline design solution is necessary, before an accurate cost estimate can be established and that cannot be answered in consultation with the appropriate specialists.

The draft policy is not a document produced by one or two individuals for the subsequent guidance of many others. It is a document which is produced, ideally, in discussion and consultation with all key specialists who are to play a final part in the implementation of the project. That they have been party to it and can identify themselves which is of prime importance for, once the investment appraisal has yielded a satisfactory result, policy must be followed closely in the preparation and implementation of the final scheme. The architect who has not been consulted in the preparation of his brief may be as ineffective as the builder who has not been consulted in the design.

The main heading for the draft policy are shown in Table 6.1. This table denotes the sequence of presentation rather than that of preparation. Terms have been chosen to conform with systems of management accounting in the industry.

Table 6.1 The main headings for the draft policy

S. No.	Main Headings
1.	General statement of policy
2.	The building
3.	Revenue-producing areas
4.	Servicing areas
5.	Administrative and general requirements
6.	Advertising and business promotion
7.	Engineering: heat, light and power
8.	Repairs and maintenance
9.	Reconciliation of the fitting out
10.	Reconciliation of the cost of sales
11.	Staffing and wage structure
12.	Reconciliation of other operating costs
13.	Requirements for working capital
14.	Requirements for pre-opening expenses
15.	Statement of apparent feasibility and justification for continuance.

Before proceeding further, it is important to clarify the concept of a completed, fully operating property. Such a concept can be created by considering a project in terms of physical areas and their function. Two broad categories emerge: (*i*) revenue-producing areas, and (*ii*) servicing areas.

These relate to the well used terms 'front of the house' and 'back of the house'. However, if a project is considered in terms of say, staffing and its various functions, this may not entirely fit the same scheme. Many staffing functions cannot be clearly allocated to either revenue producing or servicing areas since they are clearly concerned with both. For instance, some staff are obviously concerned servicing, they have no contact with guests and their job is performed entirely in a servicing area. Reception staff on the other hand, might be allocated to either revenue producing areas or servicing areas. It is this confusion which might appear to invalidate the choice of these two particular headings. Whatever the choice, the difficulty remains in achieving any breakdown that is equally suitable for the analysis of both the planning and operating requirements of a company.

Operating requirements should be classified in such a way as to conform with any uniform system of accounting. Uniform systems of accounting developed for any industry have as one aim a management accounting system which provides for the thorough and logical analysis of an operation.

This would greatly facilitate the projection of operating statements and planned profits. Indeed, since the draft policy is first to be used as a basis for the investment appraisal, the extraction of information for this purpose is of vital importance. Thus staffing of operating departments, production is detailed under the separate heading 'staffing and wage structure', and not under the heading of the physical areas where the staff will actually be employed, though implications for staffing will be considered in each physical area. The relationship of elements in the draft policy shown in Fig. 6.2. The main contents of each section of the draft policy are outlined below:

Section I. General Statement of Policy

1. The kind of organization involved
   (*a*) A sole proprietor
   (*b*) Partnership joint venture
   (*c*) Limited company, or
   (*d*) Whatever.
2. An expression of objectives as a brief but precise definition of the market segment to be served, together with the main types of customer and levels of demand within each segment.
3. A description of the marketing mix required to satisfy this market together with an assessment of its life.
4. The size of the properties in terms of space and capacities and other facilities, in accordance with the findings of the market feasibility study.
5. A description of the exact location of the project specifying its peculiar characteristics:

   Accessibility, adaptability, visibility and nuisances. Reasons should be expressed for the choice of the location in relation to the findings of the market feasibility study.
6. A general description of the type of service to be provided based, once again, on the findings of the market feasibility study.
7. The recommended pricing strategy for the project which must include both product and services. Reasons for the strategy should be explained, demonstrating its compatibility with the aims and objectives already specified by reference to the prices it is expected to attain, for example, average rate by market segment or average spend.

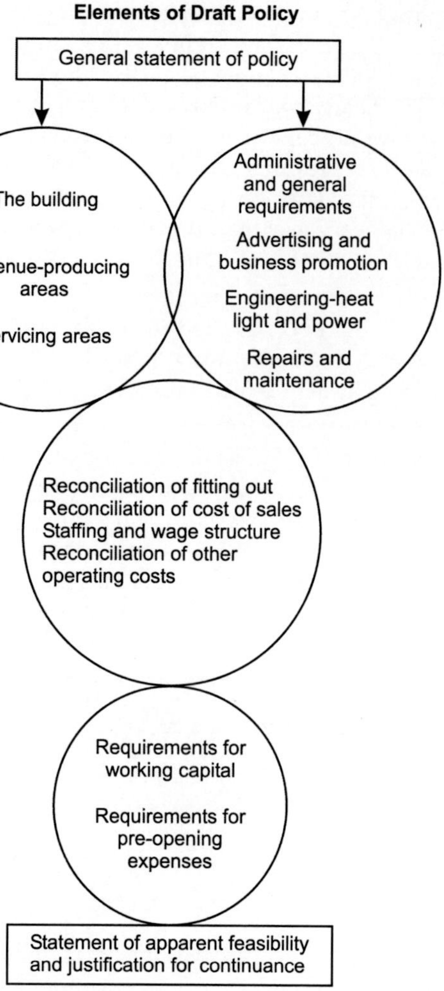

Fig. 6.2 Relationship between different elements of draft policy

Section II. The Building

1. A statement, on the basis of market feasibility, of the likely cost of the project if it is to be viable.
2. A description of the site in terms of:
   (*a*) Its limitations and opportunities,
   (*b*) Physical surroundings including roads, adjoining property, landscapping.
3. Approximation of space ratios in the provision of facilities, based on a suitable module.
4. The general design of existing properties which may provide guidelines to the solution of design problems.
5. Existing buildings suggesting the desired image.
6. Consideration of the appropriate scale of the building.
7. Construction methods which may support objectives.

8. Discussion of general solutions which would seem to satisfy the various requirements.
9. The selection and development of an outline solution which can form the basis of a realistic cost estimate.
10. A review of the planning permissions which are likely to be obtained.
11. An estimate of the eventual rateable value (city taxes) of the properties.
12. A statement of the most likely final cost of the building (including professional and specialist fees).

Section III. Revenue Producing Areas

For the purpose of the draft policy three areas which produce revenue may be considered.

1. *Direct revenue producing areas*:
2. *Indirect revenue producing areas*: Those public areas and spaces required to support the direct revenue producing areas. They would include lobbies, foyers, corridors, elevators, public toilets and telephones.
3. *Ancillary revenue-producing sources*: They are considered under this heading only so far as they may entail special requirements in the planning of the revenue-producing areas.

Each of these three areas then need to be examined under the following headings:

1. Marketing concept:

This would be a precise statement of the aims and objectives for each area, derived from the general statement of policy. This must include the anticipated volume and distribution of business as it relates to capacity.

2. Implementation the product:

To indicate clearly how the policy and marketing concept are to be observed in the planning of each area. It should deal with a description of the equipment, furniture, fittings, materials, surfaces and so on. The arrangement and layout of the area should be clearly specified. Details of mechanical services such as heating and ventilation equipment should be omitted since these are included under Section VII.

3. Implementation:

To detail how the area will eventually work in relation to the anticipated volume of business and to the aims and objectives previously laid down. The organization of any service activity must be examined according to the adequacy and position of equipment, flow of materials, staff and customers.

4. The costs:

These can be divided into two parts:

(*a*) *Capital costs*: There must be accurately estimated for the creation of the right product and the right process.

(*b*) *Operating costs* (excluding staffing): These must be estimated. These are costs of a direct nature things as cleaning supplies, licences and permits, and replacement costs for operating equipment. The effects of taxation must also be considered.

5. The implications for staffing:

An examination of the staffing required to support the prescribed service standards for each area must be made. This must be balanced with requirements posed by both the 'product' and the 'process'. Means of minimising staffing without alienating the potential customer must be explored at this stage. As with other aspects of policy, while this is a preliminary examination, the final estimate of requirements must be reasonably accurate. It is from these separate examinations of staffing for each area, that the total staffing and therefore the total wage structure and labour cost will be extracted. Staffing cannot be considered for an area in isolation, for it only in viewing the staffing for the property as a whole that organizational requirements can be properly analysed and the foundations laid for manpower planning.

Section IV. Servicing Areas

Servicing areas dealt with here are those of a direct operational nature. Offices, for instance, are not of a direct operational nature and are considered under the heading 'administrative and general requirements'. However, of the servicing areas included there are those where something is actually produced or processed as opposed to those which are merely of a supporting nature. There is thus a division between actual servicing areas and ancillary servicing areas.

1. **Actual servicing area include:**

   Production/operational areas, ware washing and reception, uniformed service, telephone and switchboard and housekeeping. As boiler rooms and engineering areas pose very specialised requirements they could be considered in detail under 'heat, light and power' and 'repairs and maintenance'. They would only be considered here to the extent that equipment and performance must conform to overall implementation of policy.

2. **Ancillary servicing areas include:**

   Receiving, storage, rubbish disposal, security-timekeeping, changing rooms and other staff facilities.

   All servicing areas having been listed, they may now be examined further under the same headings as before:

1. **Application of the marketing concept:**

   This seeks to detail the exact needs which arise from the marketing concept of the revenue-producing area serviced. Thus in allocation of space, layout and choice of equipment, and in all other respects, the servicing area must reflect aims and objectives already specified.

2. **Implementation: the product:**

   The purpose here is also to specify, as a basis for cost estimates, how the actual area will be designed and equipped. To achieve, this aspects such as purchasing, receiving, storage and preparation must be thoroughly thought out in accordance with the aims and ojectives.

3. **Implementations: the process:**

   Again, as with the revenue producing areas, this must show how the area will actually work as a component part of the total system. For instance, if it is a production centre, the policy must describe how its organization and methods of work are tailored to the needs to be served.

4. **The costs:**

   These cost can be divided into two parts:

   (*a*) *Capital costs* must be accurately estimated for servicing areas as above.

   (*b*) *Operating costs* (excluding staffing) must also be estimated. These are, costs of a direct nature. It is most important that an estimate of any direct cost of sales should be included. In the case of production this would apply to the cost of material to be produced. It could be calculated after a analysis of the marketing information already detailed for the volume of sales and sales mix, and from the information subsequently developed regarding purchasing, receiving, storage and preparation. In the case of, say, a garage, from which it was planned to sell petrol, the same sort of thing would also apply.

5. The implications for staffing:

A full examination must be made of the various staffing requirements for the servicing areas. Staffing must be no more nor less than that needed to fulfil the established aims and objectives.

The differentiation between revenue producing areas and servicing areas needs to be clearly demarcated. This approach is more meaningful than a treatment of all areas as a block or an attempt to group areas according to a conventional departmental structure. Generally servicing areas are often considered before the revenue producing areas which they serve. In such a case the revenue producing area is determined by the servicing area and may thus owe nothing to the marketing objectives and general statement of policy. For instance, it is logical and essential that the marketing concept determines the shaping of the production area which, in turn determines the shaping of any ancillary servicing areas such as storage. A total system then emerges which is in compliance with the aims and objectives of the enterprise.

Section V. Administrative and General Requirements

1. Organization and staffing:

Considered the staffing requirements for general management, accounting and other specialist departments such as personnel, purchasing and management services. A policy statement is necessary specifying the style of management envisaged and the provision of supporting staff activities that will be required. A personnel department cannot be planned in the absence of a policy for recruitment, selection and subsequent training of staff does exist.

2. Administrative area:

Requirements for the allocation and location of space for offices cannot be determined until the policy and proposed staffing have been established. The way in which the organization in planned to work in terms of management interrelationships and communications is an important consideration in the locating of offices.

3. The costs:

(*a*) Capital costs for the equipping and fitting out of all offices must be accurately estimated. The needs for office equipment must be properly related to the size of the project and the volume of business envisaged.

(*b*) Other operating costs must also be estimated. They include such diverse items as office supplies, provision for bad debts, insurance, postage, consulting, licences and permits and so on.

Section VI. Advertising and Business Promotion

1. Organization and staffing:

A policy statement with regard to advertising and business promotion is essential. It should be derived from the market feasibility study to which recommendations are appended regarding the organization of the sales effort. Staffing requirements and allocation of the office area follow, bearing in mind the same considerations as for Section V.

2. **The costs:**

   (*a*) *Capital costs* must be estimated for the equipping and fitting out of the envisaged office space.

   (*b*) *Operating costs* include such items as office supplies, newsclips services, travel and photography. Travel, if sales representatives are to be employed, may be significant. Include a figure for complimentary services and entertainment. This is likely to represent a significant amount in any advertising and business promotion budget and should be carefully estimated.

3. **Advertising:**

   The advertising budget must entirely rely on the established marketing policy. The amount of advertising and the selection of media will depend on the segment of the market to be served and the levels of demand within that segment. Thus any planned advertising campaign may include national and local newspapers and magazines, direct mail, outdoor signs, radio and television. It would also include items such as brochures and other promotional material. The size of the advertising budget is a function of the marketing tasks to be achieved.

Section VII. Engineering: Heat, Light and Power

The choice of mechanical and engineering installations should be considered as well as their subsequent operation. In the preparation of this section of the draft policy, some specialists advice and consultation would be required. The first question may involve an examination of the most economic sources of power available, electricity, gas or oil, providing that the service given by each alternative meets the requirements of the operation equally well. Subsequent to this, further examination can be made as follows:

1. **Applications of the marketing concept:**

   An assessment must first be made of how the requirements of the marketing concept affect the provision of mechanical and engineering services. Whatever the installations decided on, their performance must be compatible with the aims and objectives already specified.

2. **Implementation the product:**

   The following installations must certainly be considered and outline investigations made as to the most suitable: plumbing and sanitary systems, electrical installations, heating systems, appliances, fuels, ventilation and air conditioning, refrigeration and food storage, lifts, public address systems, telephones and internal communications.

3. **Implementation the process:**

   The process how the installations will actually work in relation to one another, to the volume of business and to the size of the project, need to be examined. The siting and accessibility of installations are important considerations, but these would also be considered under the heading of repairs and maintenance.

4. **The costs:**

   (*a*) *Capital cost* must be carefully estimated. These items are likely to represent a substantial proportion of the total cost of the project.

   (*b*) *Operating costs* (excluding staffing) include such items as oil, gas, coal, electric current, water, steam and other consumables such as employees' uniforms, light fittings or tools. A realistic assessment of likely consumption rates would need to be made.

5. Implications for staffing:

This category should include the wages and salaries of those technicians concerned with the direct operation of installations as opposed to their maintenance.

For examples in considering the appointment of a Chief Engineer, the provision and siting of an engineering office must be considered with the addition to capital cost which its equipping would entail.

Section VIII. Repairs and Maintenance

The components of the second half of the operational engineering department are included here, and these may be considered in a similar way:

1. Applications of the marketing concept:

The way in which the marketing concept will affect the whole questions of repairs and maintenance must be examined. The development of planned maintenance programs and provisions for the execution of all repair work must be taken into account.

2. Implementation:

Major policy decisions revolve around whether a properties is to effect its own repairs and maintenance or whether it is to rely on maintenance contracts and outside resources. Such decisions will depend on factors such as the size of the project, availability of space and skilled staff and, of course, comparative costs. If upholstery, carpentry and paint shops are to be included, this will involve space allocation and siting to enable the efficient flow of men and materials.

3. The costs:

(*a*) *Capital costs* will be incurred in the provision of storage space and any work rooms. The cost of fitting out and equipping any upholstery or other shops must be accurately estimated.

(*b*) *Operating costs* will include maintenance contracts and estimates for all supplies and repairs.

4. Implications for staffing:

Staffing here will include electricians, plumbers, painters, carpenters, window cleaners, upholsterers and any other categories concerned solely with repairs and maintenance.

Section IX. Reconciliation of the Fitting Out

Once all areas have been dealt with, a reconciliation of the total capital cost of fitting out can be undertaken. A preliminary comparison can be made of the relative cost incurred by each area and this can be related to the contribution made to total revenue. Sub-totals should be shown for all those areas which are clearly catering as opposed to those which are part of the revenue producing department.

A second sub-total will represent 'administrative and general requirements', advertising and business promotion', 'engineering: heat, light and power' and 'repairs and maintenance'.

A third sub-total will represent other departments such as valeting, garage and telephone.

By dividing the capital cost of fitting out in this way a separate investment appraisal for catering is made easier.

Section X. Reconciliation of the Cost of Sales

A reconciliation of the figures representing the costs of sales can now also be affected. The planned cost of sales will depend upon a consideration of the purchasing and processing of materials, sales prices and sales mixes. The items involved are generally: cost production. By including the cost of sales figures in the draft policy in this manner, the forecasted house profit is easier to identify.

Section XI. Staffing and Wage Structure

The implications for staffing having been considered for all areas of the property, a staffing guide can be produced showing the numbers of staff of each category required. Such a staffing guide should give sub-totals for the departments, other operated departments, administrative and general requirements, advertising and business promotion, engineering : heat, light and power, and repairs and maintenance. Wage and salary rates can then be extended against the actual numbers of staff and a figure produced for the annual cost of labour.

In practice, this is a very complex question and one which is increasingly crucial to the operation of all properties. Numbers of staff must be based on standards of productivity determined in accordance with the marketing concept and strictly related to forecast volumes of business. Therefore, a pre-requisite is to determine standards which accord with the aims and objectives expressed in the general statement of policy.

The question of wage and salary levels is also important. The wage structure must be balanced so that each employee earns an amount which is proportionate to that earned by others. Incentives, bonuses, tips, fringe benefits and wage ceilings must be taken into consideration. Wages and salaries must be competitive with other properties and industries in the area. These are all factors which introduce the whole spectrum of a wages and salaries policy. Yet it is vital to consider this as part of the draft policy since a realistic figure for the cost of labour is essential to determine a profit figure on which to base the investment appraisal.

Section XII. Reconciliation of other Operating Costs

In is now possible to reconcile all the other direct operating costs. As they are based on the most likely volume of business, they can be listed simply as cost percentages by department. Since these costs are the most variable according to the level of sales volume, these same percentages may be intelligently adjusted so as to be applied to any high or low levels of forecasted sales. The requirement for further levels of forecasted sales will become apparent later.

Section XIII. Requirement for Working Capital

The amount of working capital will add to the total capital outlay involved in the project. It should be kept to a minimum. Working capital comprises the funds necessary for the smooth continuation of the month to month operation of a business. Such funds are needed to meet liabilities such as the payment of wages and salaries and the purchase of raw materials. Some businesses has the advantage that a large proportion of its sales is in cash; most of its purchases, on the other hand, are made on the basis of a month's (or more) credit. The purchasing policy should be designed to maintain all stocks at a minimum safe level so as not to tie up unnecessary working capital. A cash forecast or cash budget, balancing cash flows in and out should be prepared. Good financial management has on the ability to control this aspect of the operation, especially where business is highly seasonal.

Section XIV. Requirement for Pre-opening Expenses

Funds are required to meet pre-opening expenses. An advance decision must be made as to the staff that will start their employment before the property opens and this will relate to the induction and training programmes envisaged as well as pre-opening cleaning and fitting out. In additions these advance salaries and wages, the cost of advance advertising and business promotion will have to be met. This must be related to the overall marketing policy and estimated accordingly.

Section XV. Statement of Apparent Feasibility and Justification for Continuance

It would be pointless to continue with any detailed approach to financing and evaluating the investment if it appears, having completed the draft policy, that the project was not viable. The draft policy will contain sufficient information to ascertain its apparent viability. A final statement should be made as to feasibility and this must act as the justification for continuance. Architects, surveyors and other specialists, receiving a copy of the draft policy will thus be informed that, subject to financing and a detailed investment appraisal, the project will proceed.

THE FORECAST OF GROSS OPERATING PROFIT

The term 'gross operating profit' does not refer to the same level of profit as the gross profit under double entry systems of accounting. Fig. 6.3 provides a pro forma which may be used as the structure of a profit projection for a new property.

The top of the form simply describes the operation to which it refers, records the names of the people who prepared and approved it, cross refers to the feasibility study on which it is based and pinpoints its time status. A box may be checked to show that no marketing study has been carried out. This might be the case if a superficial investigation of a site had been undertaken to determine whether the cost of a full feasibility study was worthwhile. It should also be recognised that after the preliminary study the data have to be brought up to data at regular intervals. There is no question of a single feasibility study. A series of studies which may be conducted eventually merge with the market information system of the operating property.

Item 1 to 4:

The first section of the form, item 1 to 4, provides summary information about the average rate of the proposed product. These data are the heart beat and the pulse of the business. Item 3 and 4 are included to assess the sensitivity of these factors to changes in the market conditions. The main product of a property usually makes by far the largest contribution to fixed costs and profit: indeed the viability of the whole operation may depend on this aspect of performance.

Item 5 to 11:

Of course, the true determinant of profitability is the interaction of the two factors volume and price. Total revenue is therefore shown for each department in item 5 to 11. It should be noted that the supporting data is attached to the pro forma of Fig. 6.3 as a series of schedules. Thus a complete breakdown of revenue and expenses might be attached as schedule B-1. This cross reference would be indicated in the small column on the righthand side of the form. B-1 itself might be supported in turn by schedule C-1 which would contain the non-financial operating statistics such as the expected by product type, demand and rate achieved from each market segment, and seasonal fluctuations. Altogether the set of management accounts provides a complete description of the property's operation in quantified terms.

Item 13 to 18:

Item 13 to 18 summarise the departmental contribution made by each area. This is simply the revenue less direct variable costs such as wages, raw materials and other consumables like soap or toothpicks. A breakdown of direct operating costs would be available from the supporting schedule.

The total departmental profits produce a figure called Gross Operating Income (G.O.I.). Another aspect of this system of management accounts is that figures are grouped according to levels of responsibility and control. Thus revenue is a function of the marketing and sales effort; indeed some writers use the term 'market response function' instead of the economists' rather passive term or 'demand'.

Statement Showing Projection of Profit

Property (site):	Space:		Date prepared:	
City:	New property	☐	Prepared by:	
	Existing property	☐	Requested by:	
			Purpose:	
Projections considered:	Point in time this projection:		Marketing study:	
Conservative, by	Opening and first year	☐	None	☐
Altainable, by	One to three years	☐	Preliminary	☐ by ....
Optimistic, by	Established ...... years	☐	Researched	☐ by ....
	Approximate year			

	₹	%	₹	%	₹	%
1. Capacity utilization						
2. Average rate						
3. Revenue increment per ₹ 100 change						
4. Revenue per 1% change in capacity utilization						
Gross Revenue						
5. Department A						
6. Department B						
7. Department C						
8. Department D						
9. Department E						
10. Other operated departments						
11. Ditto						
12. Total Gross Revenue						
Departmental Profit						
13. Department A						
14. Department B						
15. Department C						

Cont....

16. Department D			
17. Other operated departments			
18. Ditto			
19. Gross operating income			
Deductions From Income:			
20. Total administration and general			
21. Includes fee ₹..... %			
22. Total advertising and promotion			
23. Includes fee ₹ ..... %			
24. Heat, light and power			
25. Repairs and maintenance			
26. **Total Deductions**			
27. **Gross operating profit**			
28. Real estate and related taxes			
29. Profit before capital charges			
30. Annual capital required for physical plant			
31. **Cash Available for Rent and Additional Capital Charges**			
Book Profit:			
32. Insert Line 29			
Deduct:			
33. Rent			
34. Corporate fee			
35. Interest			
36. Profit before depreciation and amortisation			
37. **Net Pre-tax Profit per Uniform System**			
38. Line 38 total			
39. Add line 21			
40. Add line 23			
41. Add line 34			
42. Add line 37			
43. Sub-total			
44. Deduct line 30			
45. Pre-tax cash flow			
46. Deduct...% tax of line 37			
47. **Net Cash Flow**			

Fig. 6.3 Specimen Statement for Projection of Profit

All the figures down to G.O.I. level are under the control of division or department heads. They are charged with setting and regulating direct variables costs with in the constraints of policy and it is their job to manage these figures.

Item 20 to 25

The figures in items 20 to 25 represent general overhead costs. By including them as a separate section we are side-stepping the problem of having to allocate expenses such as the cost of say, advertising, between departments. Divisional managers for production have no direct control, usually, over the running of areas like personnel and maintenance, so it would not be fair to affect their performance assessment by the way in which these departments are run. Overhead deductions from G.O.I. are the responsibility of staff managers reporting to general management. Thus the general manager is assessed on the level of profit shown at item 27, the Gross Operating Profit (G.O.P.).

The fees referred to at item 21 and 23 may refer to central office charges for marketing and management services provided in a large company or, might be used for contributions to co-operative marketing systems to which the hotel might belong.

Charges below G.O.P. level are beyond the province of the unit manager in a large company. Naturally an owner-operator will be involved in all aspects of management.

Item 28 to 29

Taxation, at item 28, is simply a factor of the environment which must be taken into account, yielding item 29 from which is deducted a provision for capital investment. This ploughing of money back into the business is not the same concept at all as the accoutant's term depreciation. It refers not only to the sum needed to replace worn equipment (which, no doubt, will have increased in price since it was first bought) but also that needed to improve and develop the product.

Item 32 to 36

At item 32 we pick up the book profit on items 29 once again, ready to calculate net profit. This section of the accounts will reveal how well the scheme has been capitalised and draw attention to the impact of capital charges on net profit. Usually, the capital structure of the business is decided at the highest level of management because decisions in this area are so important. Items 33 to 35 describe the capital charges. Sometimes, the term 'corporate fee' is replaced by the term 'internal rent'. Internal rent is usually set at a figure which the company could obtain as a safe rate of return if it invested the capital tied up in the business elsewhere. To clarify the position rent paid to a third party such as a landlord would then be called external rent. There is clearly not much point in engaging in the risk and difficulty of running a business if you could earn more sitting in your armchair counting the interest from government bonds or a building society! Depreciation and amortisation (pre-opening charges may be written off here) are deducted at Item 37 to yield Net Profit.

As a final calculation, an assessment is made of the cash position (liquidity) of the proposed project. Thus internal transfers of money from one part of the company to another - items 21, 23 and 34 are added back to net profit as are the book costs of line 36. Depreciation is an imaginary figure describing the loss in value of equipment through wear and tear, it is usually calculated on the basis that will leave the hotel with the best tax advantages. From the subtotal at line 43 we must deduct the necessary costs of capital reinvestment shown at line 30. (Remember that items 32 picks up from item 29; we are not deducting this twice.)

Item 37

We now have the total pre-tax cash flow from which to take the corporation or profit taxes based on the net profit at item 37 giving finally, net cash flow. (In practice, profit taxes are often payable in arrears so that this calculation tends to underestimate the cash position, providing for a margin of safety.)

Of course, a projection for a single year is not adequate to justify something as large as a new property. The projection must be repeated, probably for each of the first five year and then for years ten and fifteen. This involves a lot of work. It should be noted that it may not necessary to repeat all the detail of the supporting schedules.

The projection also allows for a range of probabilities indicating the upper and lower ranges which the analyst thinks the property might encounter. The middle column represents the most probable level of performance and the outer ranges are easily derived from this figure. For example, the middle range might be associated with a probability of 80 per cent, allowing for a 10 per cent probability on either side. (Note that this does not imply a proportionate variation). This approach tends to be popular with consultants so that they can 'hedge their bets' against making a mistake. For this reason some organizations do not allow such a format and require their analysts to think carefully, and commit themselves to a figure against which their abilities will be judged.

THE LIFE OF THE INVESTMENT

The effect of inflation and the changing value of money is, one of the most difficult things to take into account over the life of the project. If the larger proportion of the capital charges are fixed, then it will tend to favour the return on investment. This can be demonstrated by the simple example shown in Table 6.2. In this example both costs and revenues are assumed to be subjected to a 10 per cent rate of inflation.

Table 6.2. Inflation and the return on investment

(₹ in '000)

Particulars	₹	₹
Revenue	25,000	27,500
Costs	15,000	16,500
Operating profit	10,000	11,000
Interest at 20% on ₹ 25,000	5,000	5,000
Net profit	5,000	6,000
Return on ₹ 25,000 investment	**20%**	**24%**

This example given in Table 6.2 over simplifies the situation. It is unlikely that the company's entire capital requirements would be met at the beginning of the project, so, as further needs for capital are encountered, it is likely that they would have to be fulfilled at higher levels of interest. Similarly, inflation can change the dynamics of the market itself, and may change the relative attraction of the project. Suppose air fares tended to rise at a lower rate than the general rate of inflation. In proportion to the income of a family, a holiday in Switzerland became fierce competition to some project in seaside resorts.

Inflation may not affect all parts of the cost structure equally. Certain commodities may increase in cost more rapidly than others (we have had the example of oil and food) and it may be some time before the situation balances out. This can lead to further difficulties due to the time-lag associated with changes in the tax structure. Thus once again we had a situation in which companies, in a weak trading position generally, are heavily taxed on their supposed 'holding gains' from inventory. Their closing stocks has become worth much more than their opening stocks (because of inflation) and the increase is taxed as a kind of 'profit'.

The life of the investment in terms of its marketing base is another questions. In this case we are concerned with identifying the period over which the project will live and die, because at the end we have to decide what else to do with the building or the site. The investment therefore has to be justified within this period. Alternatively we could be concerned with a longer-term situation where further investments will be needed from time to time to modify the product so as to extend its life. As an therefore be concerned with being able to effect these changes while retaining the viability of the project. This may be very difficult if some provision for future decisions is not allowed for when the project is initiated.

REVIEW QUESTIONS

1. (*a*) Define the term Investment.

   (*b*) Which are the important consideration in deciding investment on a project?
2. Explain the six critical areas of investment decisions.
3. Draw a format for projecting profit of a business.
4. Describe different methods and sources of financing a project.

Chapter 7

PROFIT PLANNING AND DIVIDEND DECISION

Cost volume profit analysis is an effective tool in the hands of management to analyse and study the relationship between volume, cost, prices and profit. It is a device used to find out the profitability at different levels of activity. This technique, in brief, helps the management to know the answers to various questions like:

1. What should be the sales volume to avoid losses?
2. What should be the required sales volume to earn a **target profit**?
3. What will be the effect of changes in **prices, costs,** and **volume** on **profits**?
4. What will be the effect of change in sales mix on profits?
5. What will be the new BEP (Break Even Point) under above conditions (3) and (4)?
6. Which product is more profitable and which are the least?

Cost Volume Profit Analysis

CVP is a tool commonly used in the manufacturing and service industries. The CVP analysis is presented in two forms:

1. The Graphic form
2. CVP Analysis formulas.

1. Graphic Form

This method could be used in preparing an annual projected budget, form which variations are revealed in costs, revenues and profitability which may occur due to fluctuations from a projected volume of business. It is established in a graphic form the framework and general parameters of the operation.

2. CVP Analysis Formulas

Various formulas can be used on and as needed basis weekly, monthly, quarterly, or in a crisis—for on going decision making in order to maintain or increase profitability. This method assists in making well-conceived financial management decisions with in the existing frame work. To apply this method, one requires a through working knowledge of the operation plus the monthly and the last yearly profit and loss statements.

The Break Even Analysis

This is the most important, well known form of CVP analysis. Break even analysis establishes a relationship between revenue and cost with respect to volume. It indicates the level of sales at which costs and revenues are in perfect equilibrium. It shows a point at which there is neither a profit nor loss.

IDENTIFICATION OF COST BEHAVIOUR

The procedure used in CVP analysis is to identify cost of operation as key relate to revenue in order to facilate financial decision making. CVP analysis is used first as a planning and forecasting tool and then as a monitoring and correcting tool. All revenue is received as a result of spending money.

Fixed Costs

From operation experience you will observe that some costs are incurred which are totally unresponsive to changes in volume such as interest expense, utilities, payable skeletal preparation and service staff, salary, property taxes, rent (if paid fixed amount rather than a percentage of sales), legal and accounting fees, repair and maintenance expenses, and music and entertainment expenses. These expenses are fixed costs. This is a committed money, and if any number of customers walked in your business, you would still have at least these costs in the same rupee amounts.

Variable Costs

Costs which are proportionately responsive to change in volume are variable costs, such as raw material cost, beverage cost, additional starting over and above the skeletal crew costs and franchise fees based on volume of sales.

Semi-Variable Costs

In addition to fixed and variable costs, there are semi-variable costs or those items which are composed of partly fixed and party variable costs. Payroll on a whole is considered a semi-variable cost, but hotels do away with semi-variable cost by breaking them down into the fixed and variable components as is done with skeletal crew (fixed) and additional personnel needed as additional business walks through the door (variable).

Therefore we could classify costs between fixed and variable. Table 7.1 lists the break-down for a typical restaurant. We may modify the figure in order to meet the peculiar needs of an operation. Since revenues represent the other component to drive profitability, we will induce revenue items also. Revenues which are proportional to volume are variable. Revenues received such as store rentals, dues etc., (whether few or many customers) are termed as fixed.

Table 7.1. Classification of Revenue and Expenses as to Fixed and Variable Portions in a Hotel Business

S. No.	Items/Head	Fixed	Variable
1.	**Sales (Revenues)**		
	Food	–	All
	Beverage	–	All
	Miscellaneous	–	All
	(Candy cigars Magazines etc)	–	All
2. 3. 4.	**Vending Revenue** **Public Room Rentals** **Shop Space Rentals**	Fixed annual amount	Rental portion based upon a percentage of sales agreement.
5. 6.	**Membership Dues** **Cost of Sales** Food cost (after credit for employees meals)	All –	– All
	Beverage cost	–	All
7.	**Departmental Expenses** **Payroll**	Skeletal Staff: Manager Cook Bus Boy Hostess Barlender Waiteress Diswarhers Cashiers Bank keepers Repairman	Those additional employees needed to fill out staff as more customer walk in the hotel than the skeletal crew can handle.
	Payroll Taxes and Employees Benefits	For Skeletal Crew	For Additional Employees
	Music and Entertainment	All Since funds are already committed prior to knowing how many customers will shop up	– –
	Laundry	All Amount To outfit skeletal crew and cover all tables initially	Uniform for additional employees and all guest napkins and table lenins over and above fixed amount.

Cont.....

	China Glassware Silver and Lenin	Probably 80% of total annual cost	Probably 20% of total annual cost due to breakage factor
	Cleaning and Cleaning supplies	Probably 80% of total annual cost	Probably 10% of total annual cost
	Paper Supplies	–	All
	Menus, Printing, Stationery	All	–
	Kitchen Fuel	All	–
8.	**Administrative and General**	Vartually all	
9.	**Advertising and Promotion**	All but franchise fee based upon a percentage of sales agreement.	Franchise fees (if any), based upon a percentage of sales agreement.
10.	**Repair and Maintenance**	Virtually All	–
11.	**Utilities**	Virtually All (if decision is made to open more or fewer hours this could change in the amount but would have no effect on member of customers served)	–
12.	**Occupational Costs** Rent	All fixed rupee amount	Only the amount which is based upon a percentage of sales.
	Property Insurance	All	–
	Property Taxes	All	
	Interest	All	
	Depreciation	All	
13.	**Profit or Loss**	–	Absolutely

The Break even point will be reached when sufficient units are sold creating a revenue which covers total cost (fixed as well as variable). For a single product firm it is easy to ascertain the variable cost and fixed cost per unit. (Ref. Fig. 7.1)

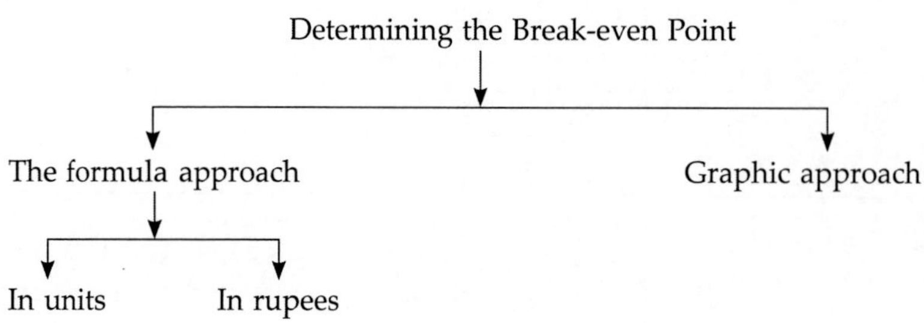

Fig. 7.1 Determining the break-even analysis point

The assumptions outlined above may limit the utility of BEA. It suffers from the following limitations:

1. Separation of costs into fixed and variable may not be an easy job. Sometimes it may be rather impossible.
2. Total fixed cost may not remain fixed over the entire range of production-levels.
3. Constant selling price and linear relationship between sales volume and variable costs is rather unrealistic.
4. BEA is of little use in case of multi-product company.

BEP is conditioned by several assumptions, important among them are:

(*i*) Total cost is separable into fixed and variable.
(*ii*) Total fixed costs remain fixed upto a level of activity.
(*iii*) Total variable costs vary in direct proportion to sales.
(*iv*) Selling price per unit remains constant.
(*v*) Variable cost per unit remains constant.
(*vi*) Firm manufactures or sells one product or in case of a multi-product company the sales mix does not change.

Contribution:

Selling price per unit – Variable cost per unit = Contribution per unit

Contribution per unit × No. of units sold = Total contribution

Total contribution – Fixed cost = Profit

BEP can be ascertained by dividing fixed cost by contribution per unit.

$$Q = BEP = \frac{\text{Fixed Asset}}{S - V \text{ (contribution per unit)}}$$

F = Fixed cost

S = Selling prince per unit

V = Variable cost per unit.

Illustration 7.1

A company produces a single product. The selling price per unit is ₹ 20, variable cost is ₹ 12. Annual fixed costs are estimated at ₹ 1,60,000.

Find out the BEP.

Solution:

Calculation of BEP

$$\text{Contribution} = S - V = 20 - 12 = ₹\ 8$$

$$= \frac{FC}{\text{Contribution}} = \frac{1,60,000}{8} = 20,000 \text{ units}$$

At 20,000 sales level:

Total Revenue:	20,000 × 20 =	₹ 4,00,000
Less: Variable cost		2,40,000
Contribution		1,60,000

Total Fixed cost 1,60,000

Profit Nil

In Rupees:

$$\text{BEP}\ (₹) = \frac{\text{Fixed cost}}{1 - \frac{V}{S}} \quad \text{or} \quad \frac{\text{Fixed cost}}{\text{P/V ratio}}$$

F = Fixed Ratio

V = Variable Cost

S = Selling Price

P/V Ratio is defined as $\frac{\text{Contribution}}{\text{Sales}} \times 100$

$$\text{BEP}\ (₹) = \frac{1,60,000}{1-\frac{12}{20}} = \frac{1,60,000}{\frac{8}{20}} = \frac{\overset{2}{\cancel{1,60,000}} \times 20}{\cancel{8}} = 4,00,000 \text{ Sales Volume.}$$

Illustration 7.2

Sales and profits of M/s Global Corporation Lahore for previous year current and year are given below:

Sales and Profit

Year	Sales	Profits
Previous years	₹ 10,00,000	₹ 1,00,000
Current year	₹ 15,00,000	₹ 2,00,000

Find out

(*i*) The break-even sales

(*ii*) Sales volume to earn a profit of ₹ 4,00,000, and

(*iii*) Profit when sales are ₹ 12,00,000.

Solution:

(*i*) Calculation of Break-even sales

	Sales	Profit	Total Cost
Sales – Profit = Cost of sales	₹ 10,00,000	– ₹ 1,00,000	= ₹ 9,00,000
	₹ 15,00,000	– ₹ 2,00,000	= ₹ 13,00,000.

Incremental sales are ₹ 5,00,000 (15,00,000 – 10,00,000) and corresponding increase in cost of sales is ₹ 4,00,000 (13,00,000 – 9,00,000).

Since only variable costs vary (fixed remained constant), the ratio of variable cost to sales is

$$\frac{4,00,000 \times 1,00,000}{5,00,000} = 80\%.$$

Therefore, 80% of sales in previous year = ₹ 8,00,000 will be Variable costs.

Total cost being ₹ 9,00,000. Hence, Fixed cost = ₹ 1,00,000.

Now we see,

Sales	Costs		Profit
	V	Fixed	
₹ 10,00,000	8,00,000	1,00,000	1,00,000

Sales – VC – Contribution

$$10,00,000 - 8,00,000 = ₹\ 2,00,000$$

$$\frac{\text{Contribution}}{\text{Sales}} \times 100 = \text{P/V ratio}$$

Hence,

$$\frac{2,00,000}{10,00,000} \times 100 = 20\%$$

$$\text{BEP in ₹} = \frac{\text{Fixed cost}}{\text{P/V Ratio}} = \frac{1,00,000}{\frac{20}{100}}$$

$$= \frac{1,00,000 \times 100}{20} = ₹\ 5,00,000$$

(*ii*) Calculation of Sales volume to earn a profit of ₹ 4,00,000

$$= \frac{\text{Fixed cost + Desired profit}}{\text{P/V Ratio}}$$

$$= \frac{1,00,000 + 4,00,000}{\frac{20}{100}}$$

$$= 25,00,000$$

(*iii*) Calculation of Profit

Profit at 12,00,000

Contribution 20% of sales	=	2,40,000
Less Fixed cost	=	1,00,000
	=	₹ 1,40,000

CONSTRUCTION OF CVP GRAPH

A CVP graph is a visual picture of cost behaviour as it relates to volume of business. This graph enables to identify:

1. Operation's fixed and variable cost
2. The break-even volume of the operation, and
3. The profit and loss amounts at various volume of level greater or less than the targeted amount for the coming year.

This graph should be constructed just after developing the coming year's budget. The graph will serve as a guide to illustrate the effects of various volume levels an operations profitability and alert you to the elasticity of year profit picture. The graph will illustrate specific profit and losses at any given volume of business with in relevant range. It eliminates the year-end surprises of profit or loss and allows you to break throughout the year, you estimated profitability based upon actual versus anticipated volume and to take affirmative action as soon as profitability steps.

The two main basic assumptions with the CVA graph are:

(*i*) You can realistically classify our costs and revenues in the fixed and variable categories, and

(*ii*) Revenues and expenses behave in a linear, or strait line function.

There can be some degree of error in either of on both of these cases, therefore we may limit our analysis by using a relevant range for our interpretation of a graph. This range is generally accurate, fifteen per cent above and fifteen per cent below the projected level at which we have accurate data.

Figure 7.2 illustrates a simplified CPV graph fixed costs and revenues at a specific volume are represented by lines running parallel to the base line of the graph (volume of business) because these fixed cost and revenues remain constant with volume changes.

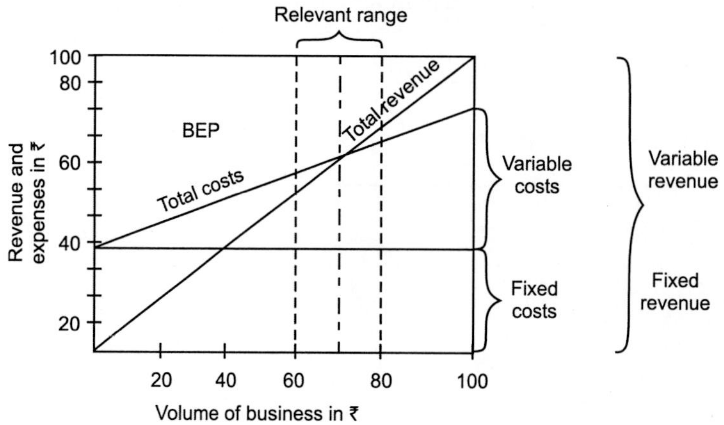

Fig. 7.2 Cost volume profit graph (in ₹)

On the other hand, variable costs and revenues (also plotted as actual revenues and costs at the specific volume of business) increase as volume increases and thus these lines rise as the volume of business goes from zero to capacity on the horizontal axis. The fixed cost is plotted first and the variable cost is the plotted on top of the fixed cost thus making the top line the variable cost wedge equal to the total of the fixed are variable cost. The same holds true for the fixed and variable revenues. The relevant range bracket is the area between plus and minus 15% of the known data and gives the range in which we can operate reliably. Chances for effort outside this range increase significantly as we move further away from the range because in actuality costs and revenues do not necessarily remain linear.

The point at which the total cost and total revenue lines cross is the operations break-even volume of business. Any volume of business greater than the break-even (moving to the right of the graph) would yield profit (represented by the space between the total revenue and total cost line) and any volume of business less than the BE (moving total left of the graph) would yield a loss (where the total cost line is greater than the total revenue line).

COST-VOLUME PROFIT FORMULAS

CVP formulas assist in on-going operational decision making. Using these formulas, we can measure the profitability of specific alternatives. These formulas use the fixed versus variable cost break-down. These items of information are necessary before beginning this exercise.

Step I. The first step is to find out variable cost percentage (The total number of rupees in variable costs divided by the total sales rupees.)

Step II. Second step, determine the contribution margin percentage (that percentage of each saler rupees which is left over after variable costs are deducted to cover fixed costs and profit). The contribution is determined by subtracting the variable cost percentage from 100% (100% – VC%)

Step III. Third step the fixed cost in rupees must be determined. If the costs are broken down into fixed and variable categories we can apply the formula.

Summarizing the above you need to find:

1. The variable cost percentage

$$= \frac{\text{Variable cost in rupees}}{\text{Sales in rupees}}$$

2. The contribution margin percentage = (100% – VC%)
3. The fixed cost in rupees.

Using the above there steps, we will set up a formula to each of the four questions which generally exist in over decision making by use of a simplified profit and loss statement as given below:

Profit of Loss Statement

Details	Amount ₹	%
Sales	1,00,000	100%
Variable costs (60% of sales)	60,000	60%
Fixed costs	40,000	40%
(Loss)	50,000	50%
	₹ 10,000	**10%**

CVP FORMULAS

1. Break-even volume:

$$= \frac{\text{Fixed costs}}{\text{Contribution margin percentage}}$$

$$= \frac{50,000}{1-.6}$$

$$= ₹\ 1,25,000$$

2. Volume to produce a specific profit:

$$= \frac{\text{Fixed costs + the specific profit}}{\text{Contribution margin percentage}}$$

$$= \frac{50,000 + 20,000}{1 - .6}$$

$$= ₹\ 1,75,000$$

3. Volume needed to make up a loss:

$$= \frac{\text{Loss}}{\text{Contribution margin percentage}}$$

$$= \frac{10,000}{1 - .6}$$

$$= ₹\ 25,000$$

4. Volume needed to make up a loss plus produce a desired profit:

$$= \frac{\text{Loss + the desired profit}}{\text{Contribution margin percentage}}$$

Now, you can try it with an actual operation which despite a contributing dues structure is losing money. You might substitute any fixed revenue you may have (such as store rental) in place of the dues revenue or eliminate the fixed revenue completely if you have none.

Now, to break-even you may have some of the possible alternatives. Following each alternative is the formula solution. You must judge which alternatives are best based on your food and operation market say customer behaviour and costs, but run through the following alternatives to determine what is needed under each to achieve a broker-even status:

1. When only food sales volume is increased:

$$\text{VC} = 50\% \text{ (food)} + 10\% \text{ (operating expenses)} = 60\%$$

$$\text{CM} = 100 - 60\% = 40\%$$

$$\frac{\text{Fixed cost}}{\text{CM\%}} = \text{Additional food sales in ₹.}$$

2. The beverage sale volume is increased:

$$\text{VC} = 30\% \text{ (beverage)} + 10\% \text{ (operating expenses)} = 40\%$$

$$\text{CM} = 100 - 40\% = 60\%$$

$$\frac{\text{Fixed cost}}{\text{CM\%}} = \text{Additional beverage sales.}$$

3. Food and beverage and miscellaneous sales volumes are increased at their present ratios to total sales

$$\text{VC} = 44\% \text{ (food beverage and miscellaneous sales to total sales)} + 10\% \text{ (operating expenses)}$$

$$= 54\%$$

$$\text{CM} = 100 - 54\% = 46\%$$

$$\frac{\text{Fixed cost}}{\text{CM\%}} = \text{Additional sales.}$$

4. Food prices are raised with no volume increase.
5. All prices are raised with no volume increase.
6. Fixed revenues is increased.

7. Fixed operating costs are decreased.
8. Fixed cost is reduced at present volume enough to break-even.
9. Food sales in volume are increased and food cost is reduced enough to break-even.
10. Beverage sales are increased and beverage cost is reduced enough to break-even.

DIVIDEND DECISION

Dividend represents the portion of net earnings that is paid to the equity owners. A company being a separate legal entity raises funds through its members to carry on its business. These members, technically called shareholders, invest their funds in a company with a view to receive good returns by way of dividend. If these investors are not paid a fair rate of return on their investment in a company, it will adversely affect the capital market alongwith their enthusiasm to invest and at the same time such companies would find it extremely difficult to raise funds in future. Thus dividends are important not only from the company and its equity owners' point of view but also from the nation's view point as these motivate the national climate for savings and investment.

Dividend is that part of net profit (from gross earnings all expenses are deducted and then provision for tax is made) after tax which is paid to the quity-owners as per the decision of the board of directors. It is in fact, one of the three major decisions, facing financial management, the other two being financing and investment decisions. A firm's dividend decision has the effect of dividing its after tax profits into two categories namely:

1. Retained earnings to finance growth
2. Funds to be distributed to the shareholders by way of dividend.

Retained earnings are the most significant source of financing the growth of the firm. On the other hand dividends are equally important from the owners point of view as it increases the value of the firm. Thus, both dividends and retained earnings seem to be desirable from the point of view of management. But, unfortunately the two goals are in direct conflict with each other since high payout ratio means more dividend but less retained earnings and *vice-versa*.

THE OBJECTIVE

The objective in choosing a dividend policy should be to maximise the value of the firm. The dividend policy must be evaluated in the light of the objectives of firm namely to maximise the shareholders' wealth which includes both current dividends as well as market price of a share.

Dividend decision is the most debated issue in the academic circles. Also firms considerably differ in their outlook towards dividends. The key issue in this debate is, of course, the effect of dividend disbursement on the value of the firm.

On the relationship between dividend and value of the firm various theories have been advanced which can be broadly divided into two categories, namely

(*i*) One which considers dividend as an active variable effecting the value of the firm, and

(*ii*) The second which takes dividend not affecting the value of the firm.

The advocates of the first view that dividend is a relevant decision affecting the value of the firm, are Walter and Gordon while Modigliani and Miller hold and support the second view.

James E. Walter has suggested a model which states that dividends are relevant and the investment policy of a firm cannot be separated from its dividend policy. This model shows the relationship between firm's internal rate of return, cost of capital and dividend policy. In essence he observes:

As long as the firm has investment opportunities in which the expected rate of return (denoted by R) or the internal productivity of retained earning is more than the market capitalisation rate or cost of capital (denoted by K), it is profitable for the firm to not to pay dividend at all and retain all earnings and invest them in those projects which will accelerate the rate of return in future. If something is left after financing all projects, this would be distributed as dividends. If dividend policy is considered strictly as a financial decision, the payment of cash dividend is passive residual. Thus, according to this residual theory of dividend if the acceptable profitable investment opportunities are available in plenty, the dividend will be zero and if the firm has no such profitable projects, dividend will be 100 per cent of earnings available to equity.

Walter's model is based on the following assumptions:

1. The firm finances all investment through retained earnings debt or new equity not used.
2. The internal rate of return ('R') and cost of capital (K) are constant.
3. All earnings are either distributed as dividends or reinvested internally.
4. The market price of shares is influenced by the present value of future dividends.
5. Current retained earnings affect future dividends. Walter's formula is:

$$P = \frac{D + \frac{R}{K_0}(E - D)}{K_0}$$

where, P = Theoretical market price of shares.

D = Dividend per share

R = Expected rate of return on investment

'K_0' = The market capitalisation rate of cost of capital

'E' = The earning per share.

Let us take an example to clear the above formula.

Illustrations 7.3

M/s Johns Corporation's capital comprises of ₹ 100 shares. It has ₹ 10 earning per share E.P.S. + ₹ 10). Company's expected rate of return of its investment is 15 per cent. The cost of capital is expected to be 10%. Company is considering four proposals for dividends.

(*a*) To keep payout ratio at 60%

(*b*) To keep payout ratio at 40%

(*c*) To keep payout ratio at 20%

(*d*) To pay no dividends.

Which one proposal is better under Walter's approach:

Solution:

(*a*) **Payout ratio at 60%**

$$P = \frac{D + \frac{R}{K_0}(E - D)}{K_0} = \frac{6 + \frac{.15}{.10}(10 - 6)}{.10} = ₹\ 120$$

(*b*) **Payout ratio at 40%** $$P = \frac{4 + \frac{.15}{.10}(10-4)}{.10} = ₹\ 130$$

(*c*) **Payout ratio at 20%** $$P = \frac{2 + \frac{.15}{.10}(10-2)}{.10} = ₹\ 140$$

(*d*) **No dividend pay** $$P = \frac{0 + \frac{.15}{.10}(10-0)}{.10} = ₹\ 150.$$

It is clear that situation (*d*) leads to maximisation of share-holders' wealth. In nutshell it is suggests that so long as R is greater then K_0, retention of earnings leads to increased share price as the company has proposal where from it can earn more than what its shareholders expect to receive from an alternative investment elsewhere. Walter suggests different dividend policies for different firms:

1. **Growth Firms:**

   These are the firms which have R greater than K_0. In other words these firms have ample opportunities for profitable investment. These firms are able to re-invest retained earnings at a rate together than the average rate prevailing in the industry or market. These firms must retain all earnings and pay no divided to maximise share-holders's wealth.

2. **Normal Firms:**

   A large number of firms may be normal firms, where $K_0 = R$. In such a case the dividend will have no impact on the share price for, example:

$$\text{EPS} = 10$$
$$\text{DPS} = 6/4/2/0$$
$$R = 10\%$$
$$K_0 = 10\%$$
$$P = \frac{6 + \frac{.10}{.10}(10-6)}{.10} = 100$$
$$P = \frac{4 + \frac{.10}{.10}(10-4)}{.10} = 100.$$

   In each case it would be hundred whether dividend per share (DPS) is ₹ 6, 4, 2, zero.

3. **Declining Firms:**

   The value of the share will be maximum when these firms have R less than K_0, pay 100% of EPS as dividend.

   For example: if in the above case the rate of return on investment goes down to 5% then

$$\text{EPS} = ₹\ 10 - \text{DPS} : 6, 4, 2, 0.$$
$$R = 5\%$$
$$K_0 = 10\%$$

$$P = \frac{6 + \frac{.5}{.10}(10 - 6)}{.10} = 80$$

$$P = \frac{4 + \frac{.5}{.10}(10 - 4)}{.10} = 70$$

$$P = \frac{2 + \frac{.5}{.10}(10 - 2)}{.10} = 60$$

$$P = \frac{0 + \frac{.5}{.10}(10 - 0)}{.10} = 50.$$

Thus, it would be desirable in such a situation to pay 100% of earning as dividend.

Walter's approach provides a theoretical background to dividend decision. In practice, however, dividend decision is affected by a variety of other factors which will be discussed later. The Walter's approach is generally criticised on the following grounds:

1. The critical assumption that the investment opportunities are financed by retained earnings only is highly unrealistic. In practice debt and/or equity is very common.
2. Another assumption regarding the constant value for *R* is also unrealistic. In practice '*R*' decrease as more and more investment is made. The logic is that most profitable investment projects are used up first leaving inferior projects to be taken up latter.
3. Another unrealistic assumption is to hold K_0 constant. In reality K_0 does not remain constant, it changes with a change in the firm's risk.

GORDON'S APPROACH TO DIVIDEND POLICY

Another model relating the market value of the firm to the dividend decision was developed by Myron J. Gordon. It also supports the belief that dividends are relevant to the value of the firm. The assumptions of Gordon Model are:

1. The firm is an all equity firm
2. No external financing is used
3. The rate of return (R) and cost of capital (K_0) is given are constant
4. The firm and its stream of earnings are perpetual
5. There are no corporate taxes
6. The retention ratio once decided is constant. Thus the growth rate, ($g = br$) is also constant
7. $Ke > br$. Ke = Cost of equity is greater than br.

   Gordons approach is somewhat similar to Walter's but he made two more assumptions about the behaviour of investors *i.e.*, most of the investors are risk-averters (they want to avoid risk or minimise it).
8. They put a positive premium for returns that are certain and penalise returns that are uncertain. Thus current dividends do minimise investors risk and based on the logic 'a bird in hand is better than two in the bush' the investor prefers current dividend to future dividends:

Gordon's model can be expressed as:

$$P = \frac{E(1-b)}{Ke - br}$$

where P = Market price of share

E = Earning per share

b = Retention ratio or percentage of earnings retained

$(1 - b)$ = Dividend payout ratio or percentage of earnings distributed as dividends.

Ke = Capitalisation rate or cost of capital

br = g = Growth rate in r, *i.e.*,

Rate of return on investment of all-equity firm.

Let us see through an example the working of Gordon's model:

Suppose M/s 'A Limited' has the following information:

$$R = 12\%, \quad Ke = 10\%, \quad E = 20$$

If its dividend payout ratio is say 60% *i.e.*, its retention ratio is 40%. Determine the value of the share:

Dividend payout ratio = 60

Retention ratio = 40

There $br = .60 \times .12 = .072$

$$P = \frac{20(1-.4)}{.10-.072} = \frac{12}{.028} = 428.5$$

If the dividend payout ratio is 70% and retention ratio is 30%

Then, $br = .70 \times .12 = .084$

$$P = \frac{20(1-0.3)}{.10-.084} = \frac{14}{.016} = ₹\ 875.$$

Thus it is clear that as the retention ratio decreases or the payout ratio increases, the value of the share goes up.

The Modigliani and Millar approach popularly called MM hypothesis maintain that the dividend decision has no effect on the value of the firm. "Under conditions of perfect capital market, rational investors, absence of tax discrimination between dividend income and gain on capital (capital appreciation), given the firm's investment policy, its dividend policy may have no effect on the market price of its shares". (*Ref. Miller, M.H. and F. Modigliani, Some estimates of the cost of capital to the electric utility industry, 1954 – 57, American Economic Review June 1966, p. 345.*)

1. Perfect capital market in which all investors are rational. A perfect capital market is an assumed situation of a market in which there are large number of investors or participants, information is available to all; there are no transaction cost, no investor is big enough to influence the price of securities by his actions and there are no floatation costs.
2. There are no taxes or there is no difference in tax rates applicable to dividend income and income by way of capital gains.
3. When investment is made from retained earnings the risk complexion of the firm does not change.

The main idea of MM approach is the presence of an arbitrages process which makes dividend ineffective so far as share prices are concerned. Arbitrage means entering into two transactions simultaneously in which the effect of one is automatically set off by the other.

In case of dividend decision, the two transactions are:

(*a*) Payment of dividend (this would cause outflow of funds)

(*b*) Raising of funds to finance investment opportunities.

Thus dividend payment, leads to an increase in the value of shares but raising more funds from external sources brings down the value of shares and the two may exactly balance each other. Hence dividends or no dividends share prices remain unaffected due to dividend.

The validity of their argument depends on the fact whether internal financing (through retained earrings) and external financing (incase dividend is paid out) exactly balance each other. Further, the assumptions like a perfect capital market and no tax rates, are untenable. Hence MM approach yields to the ground keeping in view the imperfections in the capital market.

In the ultimate analysis, therefore, it would be appropriate to say that dividend decision is an active variable in the determination of market value of shares. This is further evidenced from the fact that dividend payment has **"Information Content"** which tells the investors about the further profits or profitability as estimated to maintain its dividend per share or increase it only when it is likely to be maintained in future. Thus dividend declaration tells the investors how management is perceiving company's future.

Determinates of Dividend Decision

The Board of Directors reserves the right to propose and pay the dividends. Not even a majority of shareholders can alter the decision or challenge it. Shareholders have a right to reduce the rate of dividend—which they would quite naturally, not do and by any majority vote they can not raise it. However, it is not purely a matter of discretion of management to decide the payment of dividend, as there are some restrictions on their discretionary powers. Such restrictions may be:

1. Dividends can be declared and paid only out of unprinted surplus.
2. Deficit, it any, must be first absorbed before paying dividend.
3. Dividends which impair capital strength or leads the company to a situation of liquidation/ bankruptcy, are disallowed.

Proper provisions of depreciation must be made before declaration of dividends.

In case directors are found guilty of declaring unlawful dividend, they can be sued in the court of law. In fact, any dividend payment which adversely affects the rights of creditors would be deemed to be unlawful.

Determinants of dividend decision can be classified into three categories, *viz.*

1. Legal considerations
2. Financial and economic consideration
3. Other considerations.

Legal Considerations

There exist certain statutory considerations which govern the dividend distribution. Broadly speaking there are three factors:

1. **The net profit rule states** that dividends can be paid only out of profit (present or past).
2. **The capital impairment rule suggests** that dividend cannot be paid out of capital.
3. **The insolvency rule provides** that the company need not pay dividends while insolvent.

Apart from the above lavish distribution of profits by way of dividends may be penalised by government through fiscal measure or sometimes the government may put a ceiling on dividends.

Financial and Economics Consideration

1. **Adequacy of profits and liquidity:**

   It has a direct impact on dividend decision. The profit earned should be available in liquid and realisable form without which cash, dividend is not possible. A company may be earning a high rate of profits over the past several year but if the same are not available in cash, dividends cant' be distributed.

2. **Need to repay debt:**

   If a company has already borrowed funds and the same are to be repaid, earnings are to be retained rather than distributed.

3. **Stability of earnings:**

   If the earnings are fairly stable, the management can afford to pay higher dividends. Further, a company can easily predict its future earnings and accordingly plan a long-term dividend policy.

4. **Access to capital market:**

   A firm having an easy access to capital market can afford to follow a liberal dividend policy as it would not be difficult for the company to raise funds whenever needed.

5. **Restrictions in debt contracts:**

   If a company has borrowings in its capital structure, then there may be certain restrictions in the debt contracts such as future dividends to be paid only out of future profits generated after signing the indenture or dividends not be paid if the working capital amount falls below a particular level etc.

6. **Rate of asset expansion:**

   If the company's rate of asset expansion in the immediate near future is high, it may need more to retain than to disburse.

7. **Desire to retain control:**

   The management may not like to dilute control by raising further sums by equity rather it may retain more of its earnings to financial internal growth.

Other Considerations

Age of the company, *i.e.*, newly set up companies may not be able to pay a higher rate of dividend in earlier years of their operation.

Size of the company, prevailing customs in an industry, historical record of a company, are some other factors that my affected dividend decision.

Prof. S Florence has pointed out three main principles which underline dividend policies of companies in U.K. These are:

(*i*) The policy of required rate of return

(*ii*) The policy of fair allocation (a specified proportion is considered to be fair between dividends and reserves)

(*iii*) The policy of dividend rate stability.

TYPES OF DIVIDEND POLICIES

Dividend Policy Decisions

Types of dividend policies pursued: A fundamental relation observed in dividend policy is the wide-spread tendency of companies to pursue a relativity stable dividend policy. Most companies try to maintain a target dividend per share. However dividend increase with a lag after earning rise. Dividends are increased only when the earning become certain and permanent. Once dividend rate is increased, the companies then try to maintain that rate (Refer Fig. 7.3).

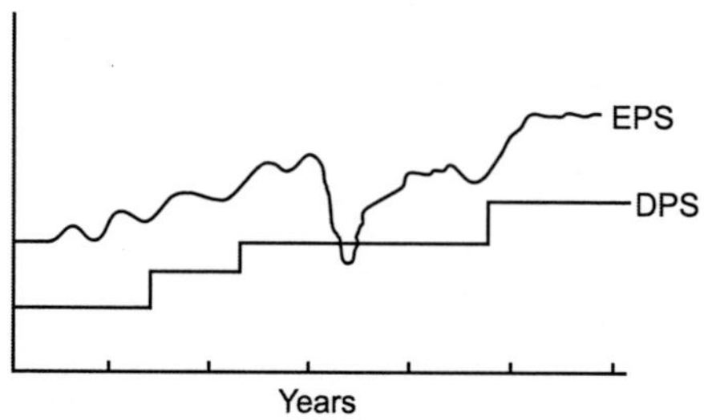

Fig. 7.3 Earning per share – Dividend per share

It is argued that stable dividend policy leads to higher share prices than do other policies. No evidence exists to support this thesis, yet it is believed on logical grounds *i.e.,*

(*i*) Investors may place more value of such shares as provided them with certain dividends (stable) than uncertain ones.

(*ii*) Many investors may be depending on the income received form dividends and they would be greatly inconvenienced by fluctuating dividends. Further it attracts other companies to invest in a company paying stable dividends. Listing of securities become easy in case of stable dividends.

(*iii*) Other Policy

(*a*) **Constant payment ratio:** A few firms may follow a policy of paying out dividend calculated on the basis of a ratio of profits. However, as the earnings fluctuate, the dividends amount also fluctuates as given in Fig. 7.4.

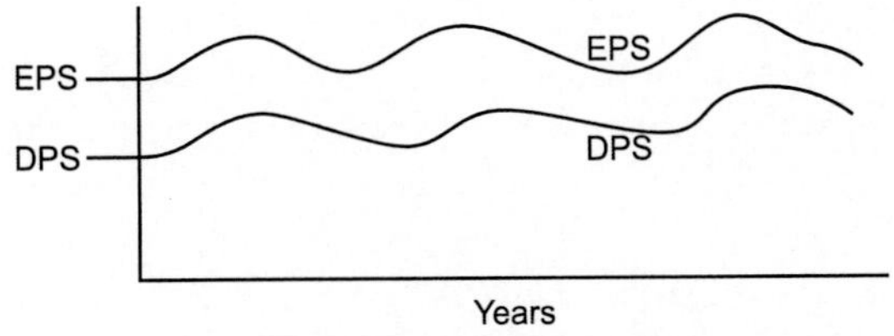

Fig. 7.4 Constant payout ratio

(*b*) **Low regular plus extra:** Some companies follow a policy of paying out a minimum say 10% and raise it above 10% depending upon the profits. However, in no case dividend rate is allowed to go below a low regular fixed.

REVIEW QUESTIONS

1. Bring out clearly the meaning of the term 'Dividend'.
2. To what extend does distribution of dividend depend on the discretion of directors?
3. What are different types of dividend policies?
4. Enumerate and explain the determinents of dividend decision.
5. Below is the sales and cost of sales of a company for two years:

Year	Sales	Cost of Sales
1	₹ 39,000	₹ 34,800
2	₹ 43,000	₹ 37,600

Fixed cost ₹ 7,500

Calculate:

(*i*) BEP in rupees value of sales

(*ii*) P/V ratio

(*iii*) Margin of safety

Answers

5. (*i*) BEP : ₹ 25,000 (*ii*) P/V ratio 30%

(*iii*) Margin of safety ₹ 14,000

Chapter 8

Investment Appraisals

The tools required for investment appraisals are: (*a*) financial models, and (*b*) break-even analyses. It is not really useful to discuss investment appraisal without first considering the tools needed for the job.

1. Financial Models

The principal tool would be a computer 'driven' financial model. The following aspects of financial analysis for a project need to be considered.

1. A large number of calculations are involved. Most of these are not very difficult and can be handled manually or with the aid of a hand calculator. The problem is partly one of volume. The projection is prepared for a number of years at three levels of probability. Without the help of computer this may take much (expensive) management time and one may be skip parts of the job, thus failing to provide important management information.
2. The computer facilitates the consequences of decisions to be examined. A simple 'what if' question ('What if the room rate goes up 10%) can require a large number of calculations to be reworked. Without a machine there is the possibly that plans will be accepted because there is neither the time nor the inclination to adjust them.
3. Relationships within the plan change at different levels of operation. It is impossible to take this change into account without a computer. It is for this reason the term 'computer-driven model', is used. This implies the used of the dynamic nature of the tool that we are using. The model is simply sets of equations which describe the financial relationship of different parts of the project. Let us illustrate by an example.

   One part of our model might be revenue. This can be described by an equation such as:

   $$\textbf{Revenue} = \textbf{Capacity} \times \textbf{Rate}$$

We would have a series of such equations to represent the revenue from each market segment. The equation for heat, light and power might look like this.

$$HLP = 4378.2 + (0.045 \times Revenue)$$

Thus equation describe a linear (straight line) relationship between HLP and revenue. This might be the case if we recall that HLP is a semi-fixed cost, that is it varies with capacity but not at the same rate. In practice the relationship might not be so straight forward and we would have to find that equation which best describes it.

4. Sensitivity of the operation to changes in revenue and cost can be examined. Which is difficult without a model? We cannot simply change price without allowing for corresponding changes within the market. To change one level of cost may imply changes in other costs.

We use the computer in two ways. *Firstly* it is used to analyse the statistical relationship between various levels of revenue and cost. It will produce the less obvious equations such as the one for HLP, a process that is referred to as constructing the control model. The *secondly* application in using it to do the calculations themselves and print out the management accounts. It will calculate the investment appraisal as a by-product.

A firm of management consultants employed to carry out the feasibility study, will almost certainly have access to a computer for this kind of work. They are doing it all the time. The individual business should have access to such facilities, in order to make use of the model once or twice a year when it does its profit planning. A large business might pay a computer bureau to provide it with a model, or a smaller unit might purchase a desk-top computer capable of doing the job at a fixed change. If does not write its own programs then these would also have to be purchased. The cost may be high. It must be remembered that whatever the size of the planned project, the cost of a badly prepared feasibility study and investment appraisal remains constant may result in the loss of some or all of the investment.

2. Break-even Charts

The break-even chart is a good example of to assess an investment. It is used in the early stages of a project to determine the break-even point,—the point at which the business makes neither a profit or a loss.

The BEC chart is a graph on which are plotted, in linear form, the fixed and variable costs of the property plus the revenue. In practice the assumptions associated with drawing the chart are so crude as to render the results almost meaningless. The relationship portrayed are almost not linear, costs vary according to output and revenue does not increase as a direct function of output (for example, discounts may be used to fill the hotel). As the product mix varies in the business (proportion of sale to different market segments or various sales mixes) so the cost/profit relationship will change. The chart itself is limited to representing the break-even point for only one static relationship of revenue and costs whilst the manager is practically confronted with a dynamic situation.

Investment Appraisal Methods

There are different methods of appraisals of projects based on some assumptions such as:

(*a*) Cash flows are given and are certain.

(*b*) Cost of capital is given or known and we are not concerned how it has been calculated.

(*c*) Profits or earnings are considered in terms of cash flows.

Items like depreciation or amorlization of goodwill etc., will be added back to profits since they do not cause outflow of funds.

Some of the methods of appraisal are:

1. **Traditional Method:**
   (*a*) Payback Period
   (*b*) Average Rate of Return or Accounting Rate of Return.
2. **Modern Method:** Based on time value of money, the DCF (Discounted cash flow) techniques are:
   (*a*) Net Present Value N.P.V.
   (*b*) Internal Rate of Return
   (*c*) Profitability Index.

1. Payback Period

The payback period is the number of years it takes a firm to recover its original investment from net returns before depreciation but after tax. For example if a project costs ₹ 2,00,000 and the CFAT (Cash Flow After Tax before Depreciation) annually is ₹ 40,000 for nine years, the payback period will be $\frac{2,00,000}{40,000}$ = 5 years. Projects with a shorter payback period will be accepted.

This method is simple to follow and easy to operate but suffers from serious limitations.

This method represents the number of years taken before the net income received from a project is equivalent to the total capital outlay. Net income for this purpose represents income after all costs but before tax and depreciation, except those for servicing any borrowed capital. Many organizations set a minimum payback period to guide their investment decisions. Any project requiring a greater number of years is rejected. This method fails to take into account any of the following considerations:

1. Earnings after the final date of the payback period; the actual life of the project is completely ignored.
2. Since no post-payback period earnings are considered, no sound basis for a comparison of different projects is given.
3. No account is taken of the actual timing of earnings before the final date of the payback period, (earnings early in the life of an investment are worth more than those later).
4. No account is taken of the impact of taxation.
5. It is assumed that profits are not earned until the total capital outlay has been recovered.

The payback period is still considered is a useful Screening methods and Traditional method in situations where cash flow is important, or where risks are high (so that fast recovery of capital is vital.

Illustration 8.1

Suppose there are three projects *X*, *Y* and *Z*. The initial cost is of ₹ 1,00,000 for each of them. Assume that CFAT are as follows:

Projects
Cash Flow After Tax

	Projects		
Years	**X**	**Y**	**Z**
1.	₹ 25,000	₹ 40,000	₹ 10,000
2.	25,000	30,000	20,000
3.	25,000	20,000	30,000
4.	25,000	10,000	40,000
5.	25,000	—	—
6.	—	—	—

Standard payback period is say 4 years, the payback period in case of all *X*, *Y* and *Z* is 4 years. But are they alike? Certainly not.

Limitations

1. This method ignores the cash inflows generated after the payback period (See Project X in fifth year)
2. No rationale in fixing up pay back period of 4 years or 5 years.
3. It ignores the pattern of cash inflows (See Project X and Y).

However, this method is good for firms operating in politically unstable economies or firms suffering from liquidity problems.

2. Average Rate of Return

It is also known as *Average rate of return on initial capital invested*. This method generally takes the average income over the projected life of the project, less depreciation, and relates it as a percentage to the total capital invested. Average income is before tax and the servicing of any borrowed capital. Since depreciation is removed, this is simply relating the income as a ratio to the book value of the assets. It is widely used method, it has the following drawbacks:

1. No account is taken of the timing of earnings.
2. No account is taken of the impact of taxation.
3. It does not take into consideration the recovery of capital during the life of the project.
4. It overstates the capital invested and understates the return.
5. The method can perhaps be employed as a useful way of evaluating performance but is not a reliable way of appraising investments.

This is an accounting method and represents the ratio of the average annual profits after tax (PAT) to average investment in the project.

$$\text{ARR} = \frac{\text{Average annual profits after tax}}{\text{Average investment over the life of the project}} \times 100$$

The average investment is determined by dividing the net investment by two.

The averaging process assumes that the firm is using straight line method of appreciation, in which case book value of the asset declines at a constant rate from its purchase price to zero at the end of its life. Thus on an average firms will have one half of its purchase price in the books.

Thus average investment will be determined by:

Net working capital + Salvage value + 1/2 of (Original cost – Salvage value)

Let us take an example:

Illustration 8.2

A project costs ₹ 2,20,000 with a salvage value ₹ 20,000, requires working capital ₹ 40,000. It has a service life of 5 years. The firm adopts straight line method of depreciation.

Calculate average investment.

Solution:

Calculation of Average Investment

$$40{,}000 + 20{,}000 + \frac{1}{2}(2{,}20{,}000 - 20{,}000) = 1{,}60{,}000$$

The ARR method is easy to understand and calculate. The PAT is easily available. This is based on the income stream for the whole life of the project.

The traditional methods ignore the reinvestment potential while the DCF (discounted cash flow) or cash flow methods take this into account.

ARR can be modified to use cash flows rather than accounting profit. The DCF capital budgeting techniques take into account the time value of money and are based on all benefits and costs associated with the project.

This is very similar to the average return on capital method. The same average income is related to the average capital invested during the life of the project. This method allows for recovery of the capital from income at an even rate throughout the life of the project. The average capital invested is therefore half the total initial outlay. The consequence of this is that the return produced from the average capital invested is doubled. As a result the return shown tends to be overstated. This method has disadvantages as are in the previous method. However, it does take into account the time factor in the repayment of capital if only in an arbitrary way.

Illustration 8.3

(*a*) M/s K. Lal & Co. Limited is considering a new five-year project. Its investment costs and annual profits are projected as follows:

Investment Costs and Annual Profit

Particulars	Years	₹
Investment	0	(2,50,000)
Profits	1	40,000
	2	30,000
	3	20,000
	4	10,000
	5	10,000

The residual value at the end of the project is expected to be ₹ 40,000 and depreciation of the original investment is on straight line basis. Using average profits and average capital employed calculate the ARR for the project and the Pay Back Period.

(*b*) Write short notes on:

(*i*) Account rate of return

(*ii*) Indifference point.

Solution:

M/s K. Lal and Co.

(*a*) (*i*) **Accounting rate of return:**

$$\text{Average profits} = ₹\ 1,10,000/5 \text{ years}$$

$$= ₹\ 22,000$$

$$\text{Average investment} = \frac{₹\ 2,50,000 - ₹\ 40,000}{2} + ₹\ 40,000$$

$$= ₹\ 1,45,000$$

$$\text{ARR} = \frac{₹\ 1\ 22,000}{₹\ 1,45,000}$$

(*ii*) **Calculation of Payback Year:**

Annual depreciation to be added back

$$= \frac{₹\ 2,50,000 - ₹\ 40,000}{5 \text{ years}} = ₹\ 42,000 \text{ per annum}$$

M/s K. Lal & Co.

Statement Showing Payback Year

Years	Profits (₹) (1)	Depreciation (₹) (2)	Cash flow (₹) (1) + (2) = (3)	Cumulative (₹) (4)
0			(2,50,000)	(2,50,000)
1	40,000	42,000	82,000	1,68,000
2	30,000	42,000	72,000	96,000
3	20,000	42,000	62,000	34,000
4	10,000	42,000	52,000	(18,000)*
5	10,000	42,000	52,000	

* **Payback Year = 3 years 8 months**

Note. Residual value of the investment has been added to the investment before the average investment is obtained. This has the effect of lowering the ARR, where a residual value exists.

(*b*) (*i*) **Accounting rate of return** is the annualized net income earned on the average funds invested in the project. Mathematically,

$$\text{ARR} = \frac{\text{Average annual profit after tax} \times 100}{\text{Average investment in the project}}$$

(*ii*) **The indifference point of EBIT** refers to that level of EBIT at which the EPS remains the same irrespective of the debt – equity mix. While deciding about the type and mix of a capital structure, a firm may evaluate the effect of different financial plans on the level of EPS. Out of the several permutations available, the firm may have two or more financial plans which result in the same EPS for a given level/point of EBIT. Such a level/point is known as the indifference point.

3. Discounted Cash Flow

The discounted cash flash method is based on the concept that the future value of money is not equal to its present value. This can be explained further that a sum received today can be invested to earn interest, a sum received in the future must be presumed to include an amount equivalent to that interest, its present value would therefore only be equal to the figure net of interest. The term 'cash flow' is used rather than 'profit'. Thus the figures used are net of taxation but non-cash costs like depreciation have to be added back. The technique may be employed in two ways:

(*a*) Internal Rate of Return Method and

(*b*) The Net Present Value Method.

4. The Internal Rate of Return Method

The IRR (Internal rate of return) for an investment proposal is the discount sale rate that equates the present value of the expected inflows with the present value of the expected outflows. Simply stated we have to find out the rate which makes the net present value of both inflows and outflows is zero. **Symbolically:**

$$A_1 + \frac{A_1}{(1+r)^1} + \frac{A_2}{(1+r)^2} + \frac{A_3}{(1+r)^3} \cdots \frac{A_n}{(1+r)^n} = 0$$

The equation is same except that in NPV the required rate of return '*K*' is given and present value is found at that rate, while under IRR, through trial and error method, the value of '*r*' is ascertained.

Arbitrary rate of interest is selected to compute the present value of the cash flows. If the present value of the expected cash inflows is lower than the NPV of outflows, a lower rate should be tried and *vice-versa.*

The interest rate that brings about this equality is called IRR. The IRR is compared to the expected rate of return.

If $\geq$ required return rate = Accept

If $\leq$ required return rate = Reject

Profitability index is defined as:

$$\text{PI} = \left(\frac{\text{Present value of net cash inflows}}{\text{Present value of cash outflows}}\right)$$

If PI is accept the project and if PI < 1 (less than one) reject it.

Steps in Calculating the internal Rate of Return:

1. Take the life of the investment in years as the span for which the return on investment will be measured.
2. Forecast the cast flow over the period of years, this must be net, taking into consideration tax and depreciation.
3. Ascertain the rate of interest which will discount each year's cash flow to equal, approximately, the initial capital only.
4. The rate of interest used will therefore represent the true (internal) rate of return over the entire life of the investment.

5. The NPV (Net Present Value)

It is a discounted cash flow approach to capital budgeting. Under this method all cash flows are discounted to their present value using the required rate of return. (If 10% is the required rate then 91 paise is the present value of ₹ 1 received after a year or ·826 paise for a rupee received after 2 years.....). From the Net Present Value of inflows, the net present value of outflows is deducted. Project will be accepted if the net present value is zero or positive.

Symbolically:

$$A_1 + \frac{A_1}{(1+K)^1} + \frac{A_2}{(1+K)^2} + \frac{A_3}{(1+K)^3} \cdots \frac{A_n}{(1+K)^n} = 0$$

If outflow is also for number of years, then

$$\text{NPV} = \frac{A_1}{(1+K)^1} + \frac{A_2}{(1+K)^2} + \frac{A_3}{(1+K)^3} \cdots \frac{A_n}{(1+K)^n} - \frac{C_0 + C_1}{(1+K)^1} + \frac{C_2}{(1+K)^2} + \frac{C_n}{(1+K)^n}$$

Steps in calculating

1. Take the life of the investment in years as in the span for which the return of investment will be measured.
2. Forecast the cost flow over the period of years, this must be net, taking into consideration tax and depreciation.
3. Discount future cash flows by choosing a rate of interest, which takes into account. What might be expected by using the money in other ways?
4. The project is selected which shows the largest net gain over the capital invested.
5. Discounting factors may also be applied to profits from alternative projects in this way, to calculate a discounted rate of return.

Illustration 8.4

The initial cost of a project is ₹ 5,00,000, with in flows after tax before depreciation as:

1st year,	₹ 1,00,000
2nd year	₹ 1,20,000
3rd year	₹ 2,00,000
4th year	₹ 1,50,000
5th year	₹ 1,70,000.

Required rate of return = 10%.

The discounting factors are the NVP of ₹ 1 at different years is given below:

First year	Second years	Third years	Fourth years	Fifth years
·909	·826	·751	·683	·621

You are required to calculate NPV.

Solution:

Calculation of NPV

Year	CFAT	Discounting Factor	P/Value of Inflows
	₹		₹
1.	1,00,0000	.909	90,900
2.	1,20,000	.826	99,120
3.	2,00,000	.751	1,50,200
4.	1,50,000	.683	1,02,450
5.	1,70,000	.621	1,05,570
			5,48,240
		Minus initial cost of the project	- 5,00,000
		NPV is positive	**48,240**

Hence accept the Project.

Illustration 8.5

A project costing ₹ 100 lakhs has a life of 10 years at the end of which its scrap value is likely to be ₹ 10 lakhs. The firm's cut off rate is 12%. The project is expected to yield an annual profit after tax of ₹ 10 lakhs, depreciation being reckoned on straight line basis. At 12% p.a., the present value of the rupee received annually for 10 years is ₹ 5,650 and the value of the ₹ 1 received at the end of the 10th years is ₹ 0.322.

Ascertain the net present value of the project.

Solution:

Calculation of Net Present Value

Particulars	Amounts
Profit after tax	₹ 10,00,000
Add depreciation (₹ 1,00,00, 000 ÷ 10 years)	10,00,000
CFAT (Item 1 + 2) for years 1 to 10	20,00,000
PV Factor (annuity) for 10 years at 12%	5,650
Total PV (Item 3 × Col. 4)	1,13,00,000
(*a*) CFAT in year 10 = ₹ 10,00,000	
(*b*) Relevant PV factor = ₹ 0.322	
(*c*) Addition PV in year 10 (*a* × *b*)	
(₹ 10,00,000 × 0.322)	3,22,000
Total PV (Item 5 + Col. 6)	1,16,22,000
Less project cost (*t* = 0)	- 1,00,00,000
Net Present Value (Col. 7 – Col. 8)	**₹ 16,22,000**

Other more refined and sophisticated methods are possible to take account of varying sets of circumstances. For instance, if capital outlay is spread over a number of years then this also must be discounted to present value. The cost of any borrowed capital may or may not be considered in the cash flows. Other factors which must be built into the calculation are the residual value of assets and release of working capital at the end of the project, which should also be discounted to present value, with a project this is likely to be an important consideration and will relate to its long-range future.

The main advantage of the discounted cash flow method, especially when comparing it with other methods, are that it takes account of:

1. The timing of earnings. Earnings in the early years are obviously of greater value than those in later year.
2. All tax allowances and payments.
3. The full life of the project and the value of residual assets.
4. The full recovery of capital outlay within the life of the investment.

One of the main draw-back of this method is the problem of calculation, especially in determining the internal rate of return or where the timing of receipts and payments is irregular. Secondly, a lot of refinements are being introduced into a situation which in any case contains much risk and uncertainly.

How accurately can future cash flows be predicted?

What rate should be chosen to determine present value?

However, allowing for all of these points, D.C.F. methods are to be recommended as an additional, useful and meaningful way of making valid comparisons between projects.

Illustration 8.6

A firm has an option to undertake a project whose cash flows, in real terms (current rupees), are as follows:

Year	Real Cash Flow
	₹
0	- 5,000
1	2,000
2	2,250
3	1,750

If the firm's nominal discount rate is 20% per annum, and inflation is 10% per annum, should this project be undertaken.

Solution:

Calculation of NPV

The real discount rate is 1.20/1.10 = 1.091. The present value of the cash flows is

Year	Real Cash Flow	PV (cash flows)
0	-5,000	(5,000.00)
1	2,000	1,833.20
2	2,250	1,890.30
3	1,750	1,347.60
Total		**71.10**

The present value of the real cash flows is just equal to the initial investment. This is a zero NPV project; it may be accepted or rejected with changing the firm's worth.

Illustration 8.7

A company intends to purchase an asset which cost ₹ 50,000. It has a life of 5 years with no salvage value. The tax rate is say 55%. Use straightline method of depreciation. The estimated cash flow before tax are as follows:

Year	1	2	3	4	5
CFBT	₹ 10,000	₹ 11,000	₹ 14,000	₹ 15,000	₹ 25,000

Calculate:

(*i*) Payback period

(*ii*) Average rate of return

(*iii*) Net present value at 10% discount rate

(*iv*) IRR.

Solution:

Calculation of Cash Flow after Tax before Depreciation

Step 1. First ascertain depreciation:

Under straight-line method the formula is

$$\text{Depreciation} = \frac{\text{Cost} - \text{Salvage Value}}{\text{Years of life of Asset}}$$

In this case: $\frac{(50,000 - 0)}{5} = ₹\ 10,000$

Step 2. Determine cash flow after tax before depreciation:

Cash flow after tax before depreciation

A Year	B CFBT	C Depreciation	D (B – C)	E Tax 55%	F D – E PAT	G PAT + Dep. (F + C)
1.	₹ 10,000	₹ 10,000	—	—	—	₹ 10,000
2.	11,000	10,000	₹ 1,000	₹ 550	₹ 450	10,450
3.	14,000	10,000	40,000	2,200	1,800	11,800
4.	15,000	10,000	5,000	2,750	2,250	12,250
5.	25,000	10,000	15,000	8,250	6,750	16,750
					11,250	**61,250**

(*i*) Calculation of payback period:

CFAT	Cumulative
₹	₹
10,000	10,000
10,450	20,450
11,800	32,250
12,250	44,500
16,750	61,250

$$4 \text{ Years} + \frac{5,500}{16,750} \times 12 \text{ months} \quad \text{or} \quad \frac{5,500}{16,750} \times 360 \text{ days}$$

4 years 4 months = 4 months.

(*ii*) Calculation of average rate of return:

$$\text{Average PAT} = \frac{(11,250)}{5} = ₹\ 2250$$

Average Investment:

$$= \frac{(50,000)}{2} = ₹\ 25,000$$

$$= \frac{2,250}{25,000} \times 100 = 9\%$$

If cash flows are used: $= \dfrac{(61,250)}{5} = \dfrac{(12,250)}{25,000} = 0.49\%$

(*iii*) Calculation of NPV at 10% discount rate:

If 10% discounting rate the NPV of ₹ 1 at different periods is .909, .862, .751, .683, .621

Net Present Value

CFAT (G)	Discount Factor	NPV
₹		₹
10,000	.909	9,090
10,450	.862	8,632
11,800	.751	8,862
12,250	.683	8,367
16,750	.621	10,401
	P/V of Inflows	45,352
	(-) P/V of Outflows	50,000
		₹ - 4648

Hence reject the project.

(*iv*) Calculation of IRR

We have to find out the rate with which we should discount the CFAT. We calculate fake payback period:

Approximate *i.e.,*

$$\frac{50,000}{12,250} = 4.0816.$$

Let us look in the table. The present value of an annuity of ₹ 1 for 4.0016 against 5 years (the life of the machine) and get a rate of start with for trial and error method.

Now in this case it is 7%, the actual average stream of cash is slightly below the average hence try at 6% also.

Statement Showing Internal Rate of Return

CFAT	6%		7%	
₹		₹		₹
10,000	.943	9,430	.935	9,350
10,450	.890	9,300	.873	9,123
11,800	.840	9,912	.816	9,629
12,250	.792	9,702	.763	9,347
16,750	.747	12,512	.713	11,942
		50,856		49,394
	Less	50,000		50,000
		(+) 856		**(–) 606**

At 6% the IRR is (+) 856 and at 7% the IRR is (–) 606

Thus for 1% difference is (50,856 – 49,394) = 1,462

$$6\% + \frac{856}{1,465} = 6.58$$

or

$$7\% - \frac{-606}{1,465} = \mathbf{6.59}$$

$$PI = \frac{\text{NPV of inflows}}{\text{NPV of outflows}}$$

$$= \frac{45,352}{50,000} = .907$$

Hence reject the project.

Other Aspect of the Investment Appraisal

Appraisal of the investment is made possible by attempting separate estimates of capital costs in the provision of both types of facility, and separate forecasted levels of gross operating profits. A basis can be found for the allocation of semi-fixed expenses. Practically, as it is impossible to find a accurate basis for the allocation of these expenses, any practical basis must produce an arbitrary result. Expenses may be allocated in two ways in proportion to the space used or to the volume of forecasted revenue. The latter method is the preferable way of allocating the variable content of overhead expenses, while the former is more equitable for the fixed portion.

Cost Benefit Analysis

This is a technique which is used for investment decisions in the public sector projects.

A part of the total development of tourism, government participation in the financing of new projects as increasing in most countries. There exists, an element of public investment in many projects, in the form of grants and loans. Cost benefit analysis attempts to take this into account by considering the broader aspects and the interests of all parties, which the private investment decision will naturally tend to ignore.

Costs and benefits to the total community, tangible and intangible, are given top projects. Factor such as the effect of a development on adjoining sites, or whether the development of a project in a given location would result in congested traffic and more road accidents, or whether the provision of a handsome building with beautifully landscaped grounds would result in enjoyment for the community as a whole. What might be a cost to one section might be a benefit to another? Many of these costs and benefits are extremely difficult to measure and to balance according to their relative importance. Cost benefit analysis is an emerging technique which still a waits development.

The main apparent drawback of this method is the a bureaucratic use of this approach and the absence of a tested methodology, obscure and invalid reasons may be offered in order to excuse poor investment decisions. Such a situation might arise when the tangible cost of direct financial losses incurred are claimed to be outweighed by indirect, intangible benefits to the larger section of the community. There are examples of prestige projects in developing countries being 'justified' in these terms.

Final Decision

Business decisions may be made under four conditions as given below:

1. *Certainty*: We know exactly what will happen if a course of action is chosen.
2. *Risk*: The range of outcomes from a given decision can be predicted and a level of probability can be assigned to each, objectively.
3. *Uncertainty*: The range of outcomes can be identified but it is not possible to assign probabilities on an objective basis (that is, based on the relative frequency of previous outcomes).
4. *Partial ignorance*: Some of the outcomes cannot be predicted.

Most new projects will fall in the third category. This means that a subjective probability will have to be assigned to likely outcomes. The decision-maker or group of decision-makers will have to make their best estimate of the likelihood that an event will occur. Table 8.1 indicates how this might be used with our pro forma profit projection. The figures in each column are weighted by the probability assigned and the sum of the weights used as the basis for the appraisal. This might work as above, for a forecast of revenue, the sum of probabilities must be 1.

Table 8.1. Use of subjective probabilities in investment appraisal

Projection	Revenue	Probability	Outcome
	₹		₹
Most pessimistic	2,00,000	0.3	6,00,000
Most likely	3,00,000	0.5	15,00,000
Most optimistic	3,75,000	0.2	7,50,000
		Forecast revenue	**₹ 28,50,000**

'Investment decisions are based upon the prediction of outcomes, the confidence in those expected outcomes, the estimate of the required outlays, and an estimate of the cost of capital to the firm. The methods used to secure such information vary widely; some are quite primitive while others are highly sophisticated. In some situations the uncertainty about these values may be so great as to make the techniques of evaluating investment proposals appear too sophisticated for the quality of information secured, and management may desire to rely upon crude subjective judgements. In other cases, however, reasonable estimates of the four elements mentioned above may be secured, at least in part, and as a general rule the utilisation of such information tends to improve the decision making process. A structured format for investment decisions also tends to lend some objectivity to many decisions and knowledge of the underlying theory or variables that make one investment more attractive than another can improve even subjective decisions'.

These comments highlight the question of uncertainty associated with the information on which the investment appraisal is based. Although that uncertainty exists, it does not detract from the adoption of a disciplined approach. It is also important to note that with discounted cash flow the degree of error likely to occur in future forecasts is progressively offset by the fact that future sums are discounted to present value.

REVIEW QUESTIONS

1. Which of the following are true for calculating net present value?

(*i*) All cash flows should be estimated on an incremental basis.

(*ii*) All cash flows should be discounted on an after-tax basis.

(*iii*) Accounting profits should be included as cash flows.

A. 2 B. 1, 2 C. 1, 3 D. 2, 3

E. 1, 2, 3.

2. Write notes on:

(*i*) Payback period

(*ii*) Accounting Rate of Return

(*iii*) Profitability Index.

3. Differentiate beween:

(*a*) Net Present Value and Internal Rate of Return

(*b*) Average Rate of Return and Payback Period.

Answer

1. (*iii*) B.

Chapter 9

Budgeting

Budgets are used as an important tool for financial planning and control. The main idea is to compare the actual performance with the budgeted one with a view to judge the level of achievement. Operationally speaking, budgets are annual financial plans prepared to achieve organization's objectives. It is in fact the final process in the comprehensive planning network. In the connection MacAlpine observes: "'Annual' budget is the tip of the iceberg that has to be supported by stragetic planning in depth and operational planning. It is a function of the top management and unless this is recognised, a company would be denied the full benefits of budgeting procedure. Budgeting embraces every aspect of a business and every section of an organization."

A 'budget' is defined as a comprehensive and coordinated plan, expressed in financial terms for the operations and resources of an enterprise for some specified period in future.

Pre-requisites of Budgeting

1. **Objectives:**

   Budgeting pre-supposes the existence of some objectives that are to be achieved. Objectives are the end, while the budget is the means to that end.

2. **Knowledge on Cost Behaviour:**

   Another pre-requisite of budgeting is an understanding of cost behaviour Cost-Volume-Profit analysis helps a lot in this direction.

3. **Flexibility:**

   Budgeting must be capable of adapting itself to changes in the operating conditions and circumstances of a firm. Rigidity in budgeting would do more harm than good.

4. **Support from Top-Management:**

   Budgeting must have the full support of top management.

5. **Budget Eduction:**

   All levels of management – top, middle and lower-must be convinced about the operation and utility of budget.

6. **Specific Period of Time:**

   Essentially a budget must always be related to a specific period of time.

7. **Sound Financial Accounting System:**

   Budgeting must have the support of a sound financial accounting system in an organization. In other words, there must be proper coordination among different systems operating in an enterprise.

Budget Formulation

Preparation of a budget is not an easy task. As such it is not the job to be done by any individual. It is the Budget Committee that generally does this job. It may be composed of the Managing Director, the Works Manager, the Sales Manager, the Marketing Manager and the Accountant Officer.

Types of Budgets

1. **Long-term Budgets:**

   In case of these budgets, demand of a product is estimated over along period of time. They provide organizational long-term targets and tests of general performances. These are very helpful in monitoring the long-term strategic planning.

2. **Short-term Budgets:**

   The long-term budgets provide a broader framework of desired performance. These are then split into yearly or short-term budgets. These show the budgeted output period. Business plans are formulated with reference to this small period.

3. **Functional Budgets:**

   Based on the major functions the budgets may be classified as: Sales Budget, Production Budget, Production Cost Budget, Plant Utilisation Budget, the Purchase Budget, Capital Expenditure Budget and Cash Budget.

4. **Sales Budget:**

   It defines the expected level of activity to which other budgets are required to be consistent. A sales budget may further be split into territory-wise, product-wise, and salesman-wise. It is the marketing division which translates the annual sales forecast into a sales-budget.

   A sales budget is not a sales forecast. It is a planning and controal document which shows what the management intends to accomplish. The sales forecast, on the other hand, is a projection of the available customer demand. A sales budget needs a sales forecast, a marketing plan, advertising and promotion budget, selling and distribution cost budget and marketing cost budget.

5. **Production Budget:**

   A production budget normally shows the products to be produced during the year. It is based on sales budget. In fact the annual sales budget and inventory requirements provide a framework for production budget. It involves preparation of output budget, purchase budget, materials budget, pay-roll budget, plant and equipment budget and labour budget. In addition to the above, operating budget giving income and cost objectives, is also prepared. Expense budgets, regarding manufacturing, administration, selling and distribution are also prepared.

6. Fixed and Flexible Budgets:

A fixed budget is static and contains items related to a fixed volume of output while a flexible budget contains items which are appropriate to various levels of output. A fixed budget is based on one set of conditions, one volume of output and a simple collection of costs. Under fixed budget the management expects all conditions to operate without variation.

Limitations

This kind of budget is highly inadequate as a cost control technique. It hardly meets the needs of profit planning. It is of limited value because conditions do change and the actual cost need not always coincide with the budgeted cost.

Flexible Budget

A flexible budget estimates costs at several levels of activity. It contains several estimates in different assumed circumstances. It is a useful tool in real business situations.

The construction of a flexible budget is similar to that of a fixed budget except that in the former, estimates are made for different levels, volumes of production *i.e.,* at different levels of capacity utilisation.

Illustration 9.1

The statement given below gives the flexible budget at 60% capactiy. Prepare a statement showing budgeted figures at 75% and 90% capacity.

....Company Ltd.

Flexible Budget

Expenses	At 60% Capacity
	₹
Direct Material	1,60,000
Direct Labour	40,000
Indirect Material and Spares	48,000
Depreciation	60,000
Indirect Labour	40,000
Rent	12,000
Electric Power (40% fixed)	8,000
Repairs and Maintenance (40% variable)	20,000
Insurance on Machinery	12,000

Solution:

....Company Ltd.

Statement Showing Budgeted Figures

(Amount in ₹)

Particulars	Level of Activity (% of Capacity)		
	60%	75%	90%
Variable Costs	₹	₹	₹
Direct Material	1,60,000	2,00,000	2,40,000
Direct Labour	40,000	50,000	60,000
Electric Power	4,800	6,000	7,200

Repairs and Maintenance	8,000	10,000	12,000
Indirect Material and Spares	48,000	60,000	72,000
Indirect Labour	40,000	50,000	60,000
Total Variable Costs	**3,00,800**	**3,76,000**	**4,51,200**
Fixed Costs			
Depreciation	60,000	60,000	60,000
Rent	12,000	12,000	12,000
Electric Power	3,200	3,200	3,200
Repairs and Maintenance	12,000	12,000	12,000
Insurance on Machinery	12,000	12,000	12,000
Total Fixed cost	99,200	99,200	99,200
Total cost (V + F)	**4,00,000**	**4,75,200**	**5,50,400**

Assumptions

Indirect materials and spares and indirect labour are assumed to be variable because of their nature.

Illustration 9.2

The following data are available from the records of a manufacturing company for the year 201?....

.....Company

Fixed Semi and Variable Expenses

for the year ending 201?

Expenses	**(₹ in Lakhs)**
Fixed Expenses	
Wages and Salaries	9.5
Rent, Rates and Taxes	6.6
Depreciation	7.4
Sundry, Administration Exenses	6.5
Semi-variable expenses (at 50% capacity)	
Maintenance and Repairs	3.5
Indirect Labour	7.9
Sales Department Salaries	3.8
Sundry Administrative Salaries	2.8
Variable expenses	
Material	21.7
Labour	20.4
Other expenses	7.9
	98.00

Assume that the fixed expenses remain constant for all levels of production, the semi-variable expenses remain constant between 45% and 65% capacity, increasing by 10 per cent between 65 per cent and 80 per cent capacity and by 20% between 80% and 100% capacity.

Sales at Various Levels

Sales at various levels are	**(₹ in lakhs)**
50% Capacity	100
60% Capacity	120
75% Capacity	150
90% Capacity	180
100% Capacity	200

Prepare a flexible budget for the year and forecast the profit at 60%, 75%, 90% and 100% capacity.

Solution:

.......Company
Flexible Budget

(₹ in lakhs)

Particulars	**Percentage of capacity**			**Amount**
	60%	75%	90%	100%
Sales/Revenue	120	150	180	200
Less Expenses				
(*i*) Variable Expenses				
Material	26.04	32.55	39.06	43.40
Labour	24.48	30.60	36.72	40.80
Other expenses	9.48	11.85	14.22	15.80
Total Variable Expenses	**60.00**	**75.00**	**90.00**	**100.00**
(*ii*) **Semi-Variables**				
Maintenance and Repairs	3.5	3.85	4.20	4.20
Indirect Labour Sales Deptt.	7.9	8.69	9.48	9.48
Salaries	3.8	4.18	4.56	4.56
Administrative Salaries	2.8	3.08	3.36	3.36
Total Semi-Variable Expenses	**18.00**	**19.80**	**21.60**	**21.60**
(*iii*) **Fixed Expenses**				
Wages and Salaries	9.5	9.5	9.5	9.5
Rent, Rates and Taxes	6.6	6.6	6.6	6.6
Depreciation	7.4	7.4	7.4	7.4
Sundry Administration Expenses	6.5	6.5	6.5	6.5
Total Fixed Expenses	**30.00**	**30.00**	**30.00**	**30.00**
Total cost (I + II + III)	108	124.80	141.60	151.60
Profit (Sales – Total Cost)	**12**	**25.20**	**38.40**	**48.40**
Sales	**120**	**150**	**180**	**200**

Financial Budgets

Financial budgets are of many types such as profit budget, budgeted profit and loss account, projected balance sheet, master budget, cash budget, inventory budget, capital expenditure budget, etc. More important among these are the cash budget and the capital expenditure budget (*Ref. Chapter 5. Working Capital Management*).

Cash Budget

A cash budget ensures liquidity without which an enterprises cannot survive very long. The objectives behind the preparation of cash budget are:

1. To make sure that adequate amount of cash is available as and when needed.
2. To ascertain gap, if any, between inflow and outflow of funds to enable management to take necessary action. If outflows are likely to exceed inflows, funds are to be arranged from outside and if there is a surplus, short-term investment is to be planned.

Methods of Preparing a Cash Budget

A cash budget may be prepared by any of the three methods *viz.,*

(*a*) the receipt and payment method,

(*b*) the Adjusted Profit and Loss Account method, and

(*c*) the Balance Sheet Method.

However, the simplest among these and consequently mostly used in practice is the Receipt and Payment Method.

The Receipt and Payment Methods

Under this method all receipts and expenses whether of capital or of revenue nature are estimated and a statement is prepared as per the example given in Illustration 9.3.

Illustration 9.3

Prepare a cash budget for the months of May, June and July on the basis of the information furnished below:

........Company Ltd.
Monthly Purchase Sales and Expenses

(Amount in ₹)

Month	Credit Sales	Credit Purchases	Wages	Manufacturing expenses	Office expenses	Selling expenses
March	60,000	36,000	9,000	4,000	2,000	4,000
April	62,000	38,000	8,000	3,000	1,500	5,500
May	64,000	33,000	10,000	4,500	2,500	4,500
June	58,000	35,000	8,500	3,500	2,000	3,500
July	56,000	39,000	9,500	4,000	1,000	4,500
Aug.	60,000	34,000	8,000	3,000	1,500	4,500

Additional Information

1. Cash Balance on 1st May is ₹ 8,000.
2. Plant costing ₹ 16,000 is due for delivery in July payable 10 per cent on delivery and balance after three months.
3. Advance Tax of ₹ 8,000 each is payable in March and June.
4. Period of credit allowed (*i*) by suppliers two months; (*ii*) to customers one month.
5. Lag in payment of manufacturing expenses 1/2 months.
6. Lag in payment of office and selling expenses one month.

Solution:

........Company Ltd.
CASH BUDGET

(Amount in ₹)

Particular	Months		
	May	June	July
Opening balance	**8,000**	**13,750**	**12,250**
Estimated Cash receipts from Debtors against Credit sales	62,000	64,000	58,000
	(A) 70,000	(C) 77,750	(E) 70,250
Estimated cash payments			
Creditors (Purchases)	36,000	38,000	33,000
Wages	10,000	8,500	9,500
Manufacturing expenses	3,750	4,000	3,750
Office expenses	1,500	2,500	2,000
Selling expenses	5,000	4,500	3,500
Plant-Payment on delivery	—	—	1,600
Advance Tax	—	8,000	—
	(B) 56,250	(D) 65,500	(F) 53,350
	A – B = 13,750	**C – D = 12,250**	**E – F = 16,900**

Notes:

1. Opening balance of June is found out by preparing cash budget for May and for July on the same basis.
2. As credit allowed to customers is one month, the amount of credit sales in April is likely to be collected in May and so on.
3. As the credit period allowed by creditors is two months, the payment for credit purchases for March shall be made in May and so on.
4. On half of manufacturing expenses for April and 1/2 of May are to be paid in May and so on.

REVIEW QUESTIONS

1. (*a*) What is 'budgeting'?
   (*b*) How is it useful to management?
2. Explain the utility of cost volume profit analysis to management.

Terms and Terminology in Financial and Investment

This glossary of financial and investment will provide you a better understanding of what the meaning of the terms are when we perform a financial statement analysis. These terms and definitions are the most commonly used financial terms and ratios. They are based on Companies' Balance Sheet, Profit and Loss Account, and Cash flow Statement conventions.

Certain financial terms often mean different things to different organizations depending on their own particular accounting policies. Financial terms will have slightly different interpretations in different countries. So as a general rule for all non-financial business people, if in doubt, ask for an explanation from the person or organization responsible for producing the figures and using the terms – you may be the only one to ask, but you certainly will not be the only one wondering what it all means. Don't be intimidated by financial terminology or confusing figures and methodology.

'A'

Acid test

A stern measure of a company's ability to pay its short term debts, in that stock is excluded from asset value. (liquid assets/current liabilities) Also referred to as the quick ratio.

Assets

Anything owned by the company having a monetary value; *e.g.*, 'fixed' assets like buildings, plant and machinery, vehicles (these are not assets if rented and not owned) and potentially including intangibles like trade marks and brand names, and 'current' assets, such as stock, debtors and cash.

Asset Turnover

Measure of operational efficiency – shows how much revenue is produced per ₹ of assets available to the business. (sales revenue/total assets less current liabilities)

Accounts Payable

Amounts owed by the business for purchases made on credit. These amounts are paid by the business after a time lag that is measured by Days Payable Outstanding (DPO).

Accounts Receivable

Amounts due to the business from customers for merchandise or services purchased on credit. The business does not receive payment for these amounts immediately, and Days Sales Outstanding (DSO) measures the delay before payment.

Accrued Expenses

Expenses that the business has incurred for which it has not received, or will not receive, an invoice, and that have not yet been paid.

Accumulated Depreciation

The total amount of depreciation expense recorded to date for the company's fixed assets. On the balance sheet, this value is subtracted from the gross value of property, land and equipment to derive a net figure.

Acid Test Ratio

See quick ratio.

Acquisition Cost

The amount actually paid to purchase an asset. This includes all costs associated with the purchase, such as installation, freight, and sales tax.

Actuals

Financial statements describing the actual operations of the business. Actuals often pertain to the "historical" period before the start of the forecast period, but as time goes on, additional imported Actuals will generally overlap with the forecast.

Additional Paid-in Capital

The amount paid by investors for stock over and above its par value. See also contributed capital.

After Tax Income

Another term for net income.

Amortization

Amortization is the payment of a loan in installments. The recognition of part of an intangible asset's cost as an expense during each year of its useful life. Items that are amortized include goodwill, start-up expenses and purchased patents.

Asset

Anything that has future economic value. In addition to items such as cash and equipment, assets can include intangibles such as goodwill.

Average Annual Return

The expected annual return on an investment, including interest and dividends, expressed as a percentage.

Average Cost

A method of inventory valuation whereby the total cost of all units bought or produced is divided by the number of units.

'B'

Bad Debt Expense

Losses for uncollectible accounts receivable.

Balance Sheet

A financial statement that lists the assets, liabilities, and equity of a company at a certain point in time. The Balance Sheet is one of the three essential measurement reports for the performance and health of a company along with the Profit and Loss Account and the Cash Flow Statement. The Balance Sheet is a 'snapshot' in time of who owns what in the company, and what assets and debts represent the value of the company. It can only ever be a snapshot because the picture is always changing.

The term 'balance sheet' is derived from the simple purpose of detailing where the money came from, and where it is now. The balance sheet equation is fundamentally: (where the money came from) Capital + Liabilities = Assets (where the money is now).

Budget

In a financial planning context the word 'budget' (as a noun) strictly speaking means an amount of money that is planned to spend on a particularly activity or resource, usually over a trading year, although budgets apply to shorter and longer periods.

The verb 'to budget' means to calculate and set a budget, although in a looser context it also means to be careful with money and find reductions (effectively by setting a lower budgeted level of expenditure). The word 'budget' is also more loosely used by many people to mean the whole plan. In which context a budget means the same as a plan. For example in the UK the Government's annual plan is called 'The Budget'. A 'forecast' in certain contexts means the same as a budget – either a planned individual activity/resource cost, or a whole business/ corporate/ organizational plan. A 'forecast' more commonly (and precisely in my view) means a prediction of performance – costs and/or revenues, or other data such as headcount, % performance, etc., especially when the 'forecast' is made during the trading period, and normally after the plan or 'budget' has been approved. In simple terms: budget = plan or a cost element within a plan; forecast = updated budget or plan. The verb forms are also used, meaning the act of calculating the budget or forecast.

Benefits

The total amount of indirect compensation that the business will provide to employees for each forecast year. Benefits are either statutory, such as payroll taxes and worker's compensation; or discretionary, such as health insurance, life insurance, and 401(K) plans.

Book Value

The value of an asset for accounting purposes. For assets where depreciation is taken or reserves booked, this is often expressed as a net book value. The book value of a company is the excess of assets over liabilities, which is equivalent to total owner's equity.

Breakeven Analysis

An analysis tool that models how revenue, expenses, and profit vary with changes in sales volume. Breakeven analysis estimates the sales volume needed to cover fixed and variable expenses.

Breakeven Point

The sales level at which revenues equal expenses (fixed and variable).

Budgeting

The process of determining and recording the expected financial results of a future period, generally the next fiscal year. In some organizations budgeting is limited to financial items that are shown on the income statement, while in others the budgeting process produces the three major statements (Income Statement, Balance Sheet, and Cash Flow Statement).

Capital Lease

A long-term lease of property, plant, or equipment in which the lessee acquires essentially all the risks and benefits associated with the ownership of the leased item. Because it most closely resembles the financing of an asset purchase, a capital lease is treated as a long-term debt rather than as a rental.

'C'

Cash and Equivalents

Cash plus investments of very high liquidity and safety, such as money market funds and treasury bills. See also minimum cash balance.

Cash Flow Statement

A financial report that expresses a company's performance in terms of cash generated and used.

Chart of Accounts

In an accounting system, the list of accounts to which transactions are posted.

Capital employed

The value of all resources available to the company, typically comprising share capital, retained profits and reserves, long-term loans and deferred taxation. Viewed from the other side of the balance sheet, capital employed comprises fixed assets, investments and the net investment in working capital (current assets less current liabilities). In other words: the total long-term funds invested in or lent to the business and used by it in carrying out its operations.

Cash Flow

The movement of cash in and out of a business from day-to-day direct trading and other non-trading or indirect effects, such as capital expenditure, tax and dividend payments.

Cash Flow statement

One of the three essential reporting and measurement systems for any company. The cash flow statement provides a third perspective alongside the Profit and Loss account and Balance Sheet. The Cash flow statement shows the movement and availability of cash through and to the business over a given period, certainly for a trading year, and often also monthly and cumulatively. The availability of cash in a company that is necessary to meet payments to suppliers, staff and other creditors is essential for any business to survive, and so the reliable forecasting and reporting of cash movement and availability is crucial.

Cost of debt ratio (average cost of debt ratio)

Despite the different variations used for this term (cost of debt, cost of debt ratio, average cost of debt ratio, etc) the term normally and simply refers to the interest expense over a given period as a percentage of the average outstanding debt over the same period, *i.e.*, cost of interest divided by average outstanding debt.

Cost of goods sold (COGS)

The directly attributable costs of products or services sold, (usually materials, labour, and direct production costs). Sales less COGS = gross profit. Effetively the same as cost of sales (COS) see below for fuller explanation.

Cost of sales (COS)

Commonly arrived at via the formula: opening stock + stock purchased – closing stock = COS.

Cost of sales is the value, at cost, of the goods or services sold during the period in question, usually the financial year, as shown in a Profit and Loss account (P and L).

Current assets

Cash and anything that is expected to be converted into cash within twelve months of the balance sheet date.

Current ratio

The relationship between current assets and current liabilities, indicating the liquidity of a business, *i.e.*, its ability to meet its short-term obligations. Also referred to as the Liquidity Ratio.

Current liabilities

Money owed by the business that is generally due for payment within 12 months of balance sheet date. Examples, creditors, bank overdraft, taxation.

Common-Sized

A term used to refer to a financial statement in which all items are expressed as percentages of another item in the statement. For example, a common-sized balance sheet might show all values as a percentage of total assets.

Common Stock Equivalents

Convertible preferred stock plus convertible bonds, stock options, and warrants.

Contra Accounts

Accounts, such as Accumulated Depreciation, that offset a related account, usually an asset. The contra account is subtracted from the related account to arrive at the net book value.

Contributed Capital the total amount paid to the business for its common and preferred stock.

Contribution Margin

The difference between revenue and the associated variable costs. This is an important concept in breakeven analysis.

Cost

Another term for expenditure. See also expenses.

Cost of Goods Sold

Another term for cost of sales.

Cost of Sales/Services (COS)

All the costs associated with the goods or services that were sold during a specified accounting period, including materials, labour, and overhead.

Covenants

A set of conditions agreed to in a formal debt agreement and designed to protect the lender's interests. Covenants may include restrictions on debt/equity ratio, working capital, or dividend payments. See also management goals.

Current Assets

Assets that are convertible to cash within one year in the normal course of business. This usually includes cash, accounts receivable, inventory, and prepaid expenses. See also non-current assets.

Current Liabilities

Obligations that will become due within a year from the current date. These usually include accounts payable, accrued expenses, and the portion of long-term obligations due within one year. See also non-current liabilities.

Current Ratio

Current assets divided by current liabilities. This ratio is a measure of a company's ability to meet its financial obligations in a timely manner.

'D'

Days Payable Outstanding (DPO)

The number of days a business takes to pay its accounts payable, on average.

Days Sales Outstanding (DSO)

The number of days a business takes to collect on its accounts receivable, on average.

Debt

A form of liability that represents money borrowed from banks or other institutions.

Debt to Equity Ratio

The ratio of total debt to owners' equity, used as a measure of leverage and ability to repay obligations.

Debt to Tangible Equity Ratio

The ratio of total debt to tangible equity, used as a measure of leverage and solvency. Typical values for this ratio vary from one industry to another. Lower values for the ratio represent a better financial condition.

Deferred Revenue

A liability that arises when a customer pays for goods or services before delivery is complete; for example, a one-year service contract billed in advance. Under accrual accounting, revenue must be booked when the obligation is fulfilled, not when cash is paid or received.

Department

An entity defined for reporting purposes.

Depreciation

The apportionment of cost of a (usually large) capital item over an agreed period, (based on life expectancy or obsolescence), for example, a piece of equipment costing ₹ 1,00,000 having a life of five years might be depreciated over five years at a cost of ₹ 20,000 per year. (In which case the P and L A/c would show a depreciation cost of ₹ 20,000 per year; the balance sheet would show an asset value of ₹ 80,000 at the end of year one, reducing by ₹ 20,000 per year; and the cashflow statement would show all ₹ 1,00,000 being used to pay for it in year one.)

The recognition of part of an asset's cost as an expense during each year of its useful life. There are several acceptable methods for calculating this expense, including straight-line depreciation and various accelerated methods. See also double-declining balance, straight-line method, and sum of the years' digits.

Direct Costs

Expenses, such as labour, overhead, and materials, that vary in direct proportion to units produced or services rendered.

Direct Labour

Wages paid for activities directly related to production of units sold or services delivered, considered part of cost of sales. This does not include management and administrative salaries, which are treated as operating expenses or overhead. Also referred to simply as labour.

Dividend

A dividend is a payment made per share, to a company's shareholders by a company, based on the profits of the year, but not necessarily all of the profits, arrived at by the directors and voted at the company's annual general meeting. A company can choose to pay a dividend from reserves following a loss-making year, and conversely a company can choose to pay no dividend after a profit-making year, depending on what is believed to be in the best interests of the company. Keeping shareholders happy and committed to their investment is always an issue in deciding dividend payments. Along with the increase in value of a stock or share, the annual dividend provides the shareholder with a return on the shareholding investment.

Double Declining Balance (DDB)

A method of recording accelerated depreciation. Also called the 200 per cent declining balance method, this system applies twice the annual straight-line rate to the undepreciated balance of the asset's depreciable cost each year of the asset's useful life. For example, if the asset has a depreciable value of ₹ 10,00,000 and a useful life of five years, the double-declining balance method would record ₹ 4,00,000 of depreciation the first year, ₹ 2,40,000 the second year, ₹ 1,31,429 the third year, ₹ 1,14,286 the fourth year, and ₹ 1,14,285 the fifth year. See also straight-line method and sum of the years' digits.

DPO

See Days Payable Outstanding.

DSO

See Days Sales Outstanding.

'E'

Earnings before Interest and Taxes (EBIT)

Net income before income tax expense and interest expense. This is a popular measure for comparing the earning power of companies, because it eliminates the impact of capital structure and effective tax rates, two non-operating factors.

Earnings before....

There are several 'Earnings before..' ratios and acronyms: EBT = Earnings before Taxes; EBIT = Earnings before Interest and Taxes; EBIAT = Earnings before Interest after Taxes; EBITD = Earnings before Interest, Taxes and Depreciation; and EBITDA = Earnings before Interest, Taxes, Depreciation, and Amortization. (Earnings = Operating and non-operating profits (*e.g.*, interest, dividends received from other investments). Depreciation is the non-cash charge to the balance sheet which is made in writing off an asset over a period.

Earnings Per Share (EPS)

Net income divided by the number of outstanding shares of common stock and equivalents.

EBIT

See Earnings Before Interest and Taxes.

EBIT

See Earnings Before Interest, Taxes

Economic Indicators

Technical measures that analysts use to forecast events in economic systems; for example, Gross Domestic Product and Consumer Price Index.

Economic Profit

A general term for various technical measures of profit in which adjustments are made to the traditional accounting definition of Net Income. Such adjustments are typically made in order to better estimate the future value of a business.

Equity

Also known as net worth or owners' equity. Equity is the net value of a company's total assets, less its total liabilities.

Expenditures

All purchases made by a business, whether in cash or on credit; not equivalent to expenses. Also known as costs.

Expenses

Resources used to support the ongoing operations of a business for a specified time period; not equivalent to expenditures or costs.

'F'

FIFO

See First In, First Out.

Finished Goods

Inventory ready for sale.

First In, First Out (FIFO)

A method of inventory valuation whereby the goods first purchased or manufactured are considered the first ones sold. During periods of inflation, the FIFO method shows inflated profits compared to the last in, first out (LIFO) method.

Fiscal Year

The 12 month period, not necessarily coinciding with the calendar year, chosen to constitute a single year for external financial reporting and taxes.

Fiscal Year End

The last month of a company's fiscal year.

Fixed Assets

Another term for Property, Plant and Equipment. Assets held for use by the business rather than for sale or conversion into cash, *e.g.*, fixtures and fittings, equipment, buildings.

Fixed Assets to Tangible Equity Ratio

The ratio of net Property, Plant and Equipment book value to tangible equity, used as a type of efficiency ratio. Typical values for this ratio vary from one industry to another. Higher values for the ratio represent a more capital-intensive company, which may be good or bad depending on the industry and how well the assets are being used to generate revenues.

Fixed Costs

Expenses that are assumed not to vary with sales volume within the expected range of sales volumes, such as rent or administrative costs. This is an important concept in breakeven analysis and in distinguishing between gross margin and contribution margin. See also variable costs.

A cost which does not vary with changing sales or production volumes, *e.g.*, building lease costs, permanent staff wages, rates, depreciation of capital items.

FOB - 'Free on Board'

The FOB (Free on Board) abbreviation is an import/export term relating to the point at which responsibility for goods passes from seller (exporter) to buyer (importer). It's in this listing because it's commonly misunderstood and also has potentially significant financial implications.

Forecast

See 'Budget' above.

Forecast Period

The period of time for which a business is modeled. Depending on the forecast start month, the first year of the forecast period may not be a complete forecast year. See also Forecast Year.

Forecast Start Date

The month and year on which the forecast period begins. See also Forecast Year.

Forecast Year

Most people choose the forecast year to coincide with either the January-December calendar year or the fiscal year of the business, but this is not a requirement. Depending on the forecast start month, the first year of the forecast period may cover less than 12 months. In this case, assumption values that are entered for the first forecast year should represent the correct fraction of the 12 month totals.

Forecasting

Financial forecasting is the process of estimating future financial performance. The projected financial performance of a business is measured by using proforma financial statements as well as other indicators such as trend analysis, ratio analysis, and return on equity. Forecasting often takes a higher-level viewpoint than the related activity of budgeting. In broader terms, forecasting can also refer to estimates of broad economic activity in a country, industry, or financial area. For instance, analysts and economists release forecasts of where interest rates or stock market prices might go in the future.

'G'

GAAP

An acronym for Generally Accepted Accounting Principles. Accountants follow GAAP standards, conventions, and rules in recording and summarizing financial transactions, and in preparing financial statements. GAAP standards are issued by the American Institute of Certified Public Accountants.

Gearing

The ratio of debt to equity, usually the relationship between long-term borrowings and shareholders' funds.

Goodwill

The accounting term for amounts paid for assets over and above their fair market value. Goodwill arises, for example, when a company purchases another business and pays a price higher than the value of the acquired assets alone. Goodwill theoretically represents the value of the business's name, reputation, and customer relations, which increase the true value of the business beyond the value of its assets alone. Any surplus money paid to acquire a company that exceeds its net tangible assets value.

Gross Profit

Sales less cost of goods or services sold. Also referred to as gross profit margin, or gross profit, and often abbreviated to simply 'margin'. See also 'Net Profit'.

Gross Margin

Net Sales less cost of sales (including both fixed and variable costs), often expressed as a percentage of sales. Also referred to as gross profit.

Gross Sales

The total of amounts received (sales for cash) and amounts expected (sales on credit) in return for products sold or services rendered during the given time period. Gross sales reflects sales at invoice values, before sales discounts and credit card fees.

'I'

Income

Another term for Net income.

Income Statement

A financial report that shows a company's performance over a specified period of time by subtracting expenses from revenue to obtain net income. Also known as a profit and loss statement (P and L) or an earnings report.

Income Tax Expense levied on the income of a business imposed by central and state governments. This expense appears on the income statement simply as taxes.

Initial Public Offering (IPO)

An Initial Public Offering (IPO being the Stock Exchange and corporate acronym) is the first sale of privately owned equity (stock or shares) in a company via the issue of shares to the public and other investing institutions. In other words an IPO is the first sale of stock by a private company to the public. IPOs typically involve small, young companies raising capital to finance growth. For investors IPO's can risky as it is difficult to predict the value of the stock (shares) when they open for trading. An IPO is effectively 'going public' or 'taking a company public'.

Intangible Asset

A long-term asset that represents a financial, legal, or accounting concept rather than a physical item. Examples of intangible assets include: Goodwill , the value of a patent, copyright, or trademark, the value of a franchise or operating rights. Under accounting rules, an intangible asset must have a useful life greater than one year, and a portion of its value must be amortized over time as an expense. Near the end of the useful life of an intangible asset, when its remaining life is less than one year, the asset must still be classified as a long-term asset. See also tangible asset.

Interest Basis

The interest rate, such as prime or LIBOR, that is used as a reference point for quoting borrowing rates. For example, using the prime rate as the interest basis, a loan might be offered at prime plus one per cent. See also Prime Rate and London Interbank Offered Rate.

Interest Expense

Money paid by a business in exchange for the use of capital for a specified time period. On the income statement, "Interest Expense (Income)" is a single account that is the net amount of interest income and interest expense.

Interest Income

Money received by a business in exchange for the use of capital for a specified time period. On the income statement, "Interest Expense (Income)" is a single account that is the net amount of interest income and interest expense.

Interest Rate

The cost of borrowing money, expressed as a percentage per period of time, usually one year.

Inventory

Goods purchased or manufactured by a business and held for production or sale. Inventory is often subdivided into raw materials, work in progress, and finished goods. See also Inventory Targets.

Inventory Targets

The numbers of months of inventory that the user requires to be in stock at a given point in time. For Raw Materials, this amount represents the number of months of future production. For Finished Goods, the amount represents the number of months of future sales.

Inventory Turns

The ratio of annual cost of sales to inventory, commonly used as a rough measure of inventory management efficiency. Also known as inventory turnover ratio or simply turns.

Investment

The expenditure of cash to create additional capital. Investment can be in income-producing vehicles such as stocks and bonds, or more risk-oriented ventures such as the purchase of another company.

'L'

Letters of credit

These mechanisms are used by exporters and importers, and usually provided by the importing company's bank to the exporter to safeguard the contractual expectations and particularly financial exposure of the exporter of the goods or services. (Also called 'export letters of credit, and 'import letters of credit'.)

When an exporter agrees to supply a customer in another country, the exporter needs to know that the goods will be paid for.

Letters of guarantee

There are many types of letters of guarantee. These types of letters of guarantee are concerned with providing safeguards to buyers that suppliers will meet their obligations or vice-versa, and are issued by the supplier's or customer's bank depending on which party seeks the guarantee. While a letter of credit essentially guarantees payment to the exporter, a letter of guarantee provides safeguard that other aspects of the supplier's or customer's obligations will be met. The supplier's or customer's bank is effectively giving a direct guarantee on behalf of the supplier or customer that the supplier's or customer's obligations will be met, and in the event of the supplier's or customer's failure to meet obligations to the other party then the bank undertakes the responsibility for those obligations.

Liabilities

General term for what the business owes. Liabilities are long-term loans of the type used to finance the business and short-term debts or money owing as a result of trading activities to date. Long term liabilities, along with Share Capital and Reserves make up one side of the balance sheet equation showing where the money came from. The other side of the balance sheet will show Current Liabilities along with various Assets, showing where the money is now.

Labour

Another term for Direct Labour. See also Salaries and Benefits.

Last In, First Out (LIFO)

A method of inventory valuation whereby the goods most recently purchased or manufactured are considered the first ones sold. In periods of rising prices, the LIFO method shows a lower profit than the first in, first out (FIFO) method.

Lease

A long-term contract granting use of real estate, equipment or other fixed assets in exchange for payment. All leases entered in the Property, Plant and Equipment Detail are considered capital leases; operating leases should be entered as expenses in the Expenses Detail. See also mortgage.

Leverage

The relationship between debt and equity. A company is considered highly leveraged if its levels of debt are high compared to its equity.

Liabilities

Obligations used to fund the operations of a business, including bank loans, accounts payable, and accrued expenses.

LIBOUR

See London Interbank Offered Rate.

LIFO

See Last In, First Out.

Line of Credit

The amount of short-term credit available to a business from banks.

Liquidity

A company's ability to generate cash in a timely manner in order to meet its obligations, often measured by the quick ratio or the current ratio.

Liquidity Ratio

Indicates the company's ability to pay its short term debts, by measuring the relationship between current assets (*i.e.*, those which can be turned into cash) against the short-term debt value. (current assets/current liabilities) Also referred to as the Current Ratio.

Net Assets (also called total net assets)

Total assets (fixed and current) less current liabilities and long-term liabilities that have not been capitalised (*e.g.*, short-term loans).

London Interbank Offered Rate (LIBOR)

The interest rate used among the most creditworthy international banks for large loans in eurodollars. LIBOR is an important reference number, because loans to businesses can be tied to it on a percentage basis. See also prime rate and interest basis.

Long-Term Asset

Any asset that has an economic life greater than one year. Liquid items such as cash are considered to be current or short-term assets. Under accounting rules, intangible assets must always be classified as long-term assets, even if their remaining life is less than one year.

Long-Term Borrowing

Liabilities that represent money borrowed from banks or other lenders to fund the ongoing operations of a business and that will not come due within one year.

'M'

Management Goals

A set of conditions a business is striving to achieve. These may include requirements for debt/ equity ratio, working capital, or dividend payments. See also covenants.

Market Value

The price at which an asset would pass from an informed and willing seller to an informed and willing buyer, assuming that goodwill played no role in the transaction.

Marketable Securities

Securities that can readily be converted into cash, including government securities, bankers' acceptances, and commercial paper.

Materials

The physical inputs to manufacturing, treated as part of cost of sales. Also known as raw materials.

Miscellaneous Current Assets

An account for current assets that do not fall into the following categories: cash, marketable securities, accounts receivable, other receivables, inventory, and prepaid expenses.

Miscellaneous Current Liabilities

An account for current liabilities that do not fall into any of the categories already defined. Examples of predefined categories are accounts payable, accrued expenses, and short-term notes payable.

Miscellaneous Expenses

An account for operating expenses that do not fall into any of the predefined categories such as salaries, utilities, advertising, and depreciation.

Miscellaneous Non-Current Assets

An account for assets not including current assets, property, plant and equipment, intangibles, deposits, and loans made.

Miscellaneous Non-Current Liabilities

An account for non-current liabilities not including long-term debt (mortgage debt, lease debt, long-term borrowing, and shareholder loans) and deferred taxes.

Mortgage

A long-term debt instrument for the purchase of property by which the borrower uses the property itself for collateral.

'N'

Net Book Value

The acquisition cost of an asset less any accumulated depreciation. See also book value and contra accounts.

Net Cash Provided By Operations

On a cash flow statement, net income plus non-cash transactions and the net amount of changes in operating assets and liabilities.

Net Income

Total revenues minus total expenses, including taxes and depreciation, for a specified time. Also known as profit, net profit, or net earnings.

Net Income before Taxes

Total revenues minus total expenses except the income tax expense, for a specified time. Also known as pretax income.

Net current assets

Current Assets less Current Liabilities.

Net Present Value (NPV)

NPV is a significant measurement in business investment decisions. NPV is essentially a measurement of all future cash flow (revenues minus costs, also referred to as net benefits) that will be derived from a particular investment (whether in the form of a project, a new product line, a proposition, or an entire business), minus the cost of the investment. Logically if a proposition has a positive NPV then it is profitable and is worthy of consideration. If negative then it's unprofitable and should not be pursued. While there are many other factors besides a positive NPV which influence investment decisions; NPV provides a consistent method of comparing propositions and investment opportunities from a simple capital/investment/profit perspective.

Net Property, Plant and Equipment

Gross property, plant and equipment minus accumulated depreciation. This number represents that portion of PP and E acquisition cost that has not yet been recognized as an expense. It is not the same as externally determined measures such as market value.

Net Profit

Net profit can mean different things so it always needs clarifying. Net strictly means 'after all deductions' (as opposed to just certain deductions used to arrive at a gross profit or margin). Net profit normally refers to profit after deduction of all operating expenses, notably after deduction of fixed costs or fixed overheads. This contrasts with the term 'gross profit' which normally refers to the difference between sales and direct cost of product or service sold (also referred to as gross margin or gross profit margin) and certainly before the deduction of operating costs or overheads. Net profit normally refers to the profit figure before deduction of corporation tax, in which case the term is often extended to 'net profit before tax' or PBT.

Net Operating Loss (NOL)

The excess of business expenses over income in a given tax year.

Net Operating Loss (NOL) Carry Forward

The amount of Net Operating Losses accumulated over past tax years that is available for offsetting taxable income in the current and future tax years.

Net Sales

Sales revenue less sales discounts and credit card fees.

Non-Current Assets

Assets that are not convertible to cash within one year in the normal course of business. Property and Goodwill are examples of non-current assets. See also current assets.

Non-Current Liabilities

Obligations that will not come due within one year of the current date. See also current liabilities.

Non-Operating Expense

Expenses not related to the ongoing operations of a company; for example, interest expense, one-time events, and taxes.

Non-Operating Income

Income not related to the ongoing operations of a company; for example, interest income and sale of fixed assets.

'O'

Opening/closing stock

See explanation under Cost of Sales.

P/E ratio (price per earnings)

The P/E ratio is an important indicator as to how the investing market views the health, performance, prospects and investment risk of a public company listed on a stock exchange (a listed company). The P/E ratio is also a highly complex concept – it's a guide to use alongside other indicators, not an absolute measure to rely on by itself. The P/E ratio is arrived at by dividing the stock or share price by the earnings per share (profit after tax and interest divided by the number of ordinary shares in issue).

Operating Expenses

All expenses related to the ongoing operations of a company, including research and development, sales and marketing, and administrative expenses. Any costs directly attributable to producing goods or services are not included. See also cost of sales.

Operating Income

Sales revenue minus cost of sales and operating expenses. Similar to earnings before interest and taxes, operating income is examined when the earnings of the core business are analyzed. Also referred to as operating profit, operating earnings, and income from operations.

Operating Lease

A type of lease, normally involving equipment, classified as a rental not as a purchase over time. An operating lease must be shown as an expense in the Expenses Detail, unlike a capital lease, which is treated as a long-term debt.

Operating Profit

Another term for Operating Income.

Other Assets

Assets exclusive of current assets and property, plant and equipment. Other assets can include intangibles, deposits, loans made, and miscellaneous non-current assets.

Other Expenses

Expenses due to activities outside the normal operations of the business, for example, loss from foreign exchange and loss from investments.

Other Income

Income due to activities outside the normal operations of the business, for example, dividends from investments and gain from foreign exchange.

Other Liabilities

Liabilities other than debt, line of credit, and accounts payable, for example, deferred taxes, accrued expenses, and customer deposits.

Overhead

An expense that cannot be attributed to any one single part of the company's activities. Expenses incurred in operating a business, such as rent, executive salaries, and insurance, that are not directly related to the manufacture of a product or delivery of a service. A portion of overhead can be attributed to cost of sales, usually on a percentage basis; the remainder is considered an operating expense.

Owners' Equity

Another term for Equity.

'P'

Par Value

The stated value of a share of stock. Par is usually a minimal value (such as $.01) and bears no relation to the market value of the shares. See also Contributed Capital.

Payables

Another term for Accounts Payable.

Payroll

The total wages, not including benefits, paid by a business during each forecast year.

Period Expenses

A term for expenses recorded in the period in which they occur regardless of whether or not they pertain to a prior or later period. R and D and advertising expenditures are examples of costs that benefit future periods but must be treated as period expenses according to Generally Accepted Accounting Principles (GAAP).

Periodicity

The level of detail in terms of time at which data is forecast or reported, specified as months, quarters, or years.

Periods

Discrete intervals of time. The word period generally refers either to the interval of the entire forecast (as in forecast period) or the granularity of data in financial statements (as in periodicity).

Plan Period

Another term for Forecast Period.

PP and E

See Property, Plant and Equipment.

Precision

The scale at which forecast numbers are displayed. Choices include dollars, hundreds, thousands, and millions.

Prepaid Expenses

Services, goods, and intangibles paid for prior to the period in which they provide benefit. Prepaid expenses are accounted for as assets until their benefit is realized.

Price List

A schedule that associates prices with individual products. This list allows you to forecast sales in units and still create projections in dollars. See also Discount List.

Price/Earnings Ratio (P-E)

The market value of a company's stock divided by net income.

Prime Rate

The interest rate that banks charge to their most creditworthy customers. The prime rate is an important reference number, because loans to companies are often tied to it on a percentage basis. See also London Interbank Offered Rate and interest basis.

Pro Forma Financial Statements

A set of financial statements and other schedules that show projected results for a future period. They are called pro forma financial statements because they have the form of financial statements, but are not prepared from actual operating results. The three major financial statements are the Income Statement, Balance Sheet, and Cash Flow Statement. For external reporting, these statements must conform to Generally Accepted Accounting Principles (GAAP).

Profit

Another term for Net Income.

Profit and Loss Account (P&L)

One of the three principal business reporting and measuring tools (along with the balance sheet and cash flow statement). The P and L is essentially a trading account for a period, usually a year, but also can be monthly and cumulative. It shows profit performance, which often has little to do with cash, stocks and assets (which must be viewed from a separate perspective using balance sheet and cash flow statement).

Profit and Loss Statement (P&L)

Another term for the Income Statement.

Prompt Payment Discounts

Discounts that a business gives to credit customers who pay within a specified period of time; also called sales discounts. On an income statement, this amount is subtracted from Gross Sales to yield Net Sales.

Property, Plant and Equipment (PP&E)

Assets used in the operations of a business that have a useful life greater than one year, including land, buildings, machinery, equipment, and furniture. Also known as fixed assets. See also Depreciation.

Purchases of PP and E

The acquisition cost of new property, plant and equipment assets in a given year, minus the proceeds from the sale of existing PP and E. See also Depreciation.

'Q'

Quick Ratio

Current assets, excluding inventory and prepaid expenses, divided by current liabilities. Also known as the acid test ratio. Like the current ratio, the quick ratio is used as a measure of a company's liquidity. It helps estimate a company's ability to meet its current obligations using assets that can easily be converted into cash. Although typical ratios vary from one industry and company size to another, financial authorities recommend that the Quick Ratio should be 1.0 or greater.

'R'

Ratio

A comparison of financial statement elements in the form of a quotient. Ratios such as the price/earnings ratio, return on assets, and quick ratio are often used for analyzing financial statements.

Raw Materials

Another term for Materials.

Receivables

Another term for Accounts Receivable.

Retained Earnings

Net profits kept within a business in the Owners' Equity account after stock dividends are paid.

Retired Liabilities

Debt paid off within a given period of the forecast.

Retirement of Long-Term Debt

The repayment of a non-current liability.

Return on Assets (ROA)

Net income for a time period divided by total assets. This ratio is often used to measure profitability or the efficiency with which assets are being employed. Higher values for this ratio indicate better financial performance. The specific value obtained for a business should be evaluated in relation to the returns that can be obtained from alternative investments of capital.

Return on Capital Employed (ROCE)

A fundamental financial performance measure. A percentage figure representing profit before interest against the money that is invested in the business. (Profit before interest and tax, divided by capital employed, x 100 to produce percentage figure.)

Return on investment

'Return' generally means profit before tax, but clarify this with the person using the term - profit depends on various circumstances, not least the accounting conventions used in the business. In this sense most CEO's and business owners regard ROI as the ultimate measure of any business or any business proposition, after all it's what most business is aimed at producing – maximum return on investment, otherwise you might as well put your money in a bank savings account.

Return on Tangible Equity

Net income for a time period divided by tangible equity. This ratio is sometimes used to measure profitability or the efficiency with which the owners' financial investments are being employed.

The value of intangible assets such as goodwill is excluded from this ratio in order to better reflect actual operating profitability. Higher values for this ratio indicate better financial performance. The specific value obtained for a business should be evaluated in relation to the returns that can be obtained from alternative investments of capital. An alternate form of this ratio can also be computed using pre-tax income instead of net income.

Return on Equity (ROE)

Net income divided by equity. This ratio is often used as a measure of the return on funds invested in a business.

Quick Ratio

Same as the Acid Test. The relationship between current assets readily convertible into cash (usually current assets less stock) and current liabilities. A sterner test of liquidity.

Reserves

The accumulated and retained difference between profits and losses year on year since the company's formation.

Restricted Funds

These are funds used by an organization that are restricted or earmarked by a donor for a specific purpose, which can be extremely specific or quite broad, *e.g.*, endowment or pensions investment; research (in the case of donations to a charity or research organization); or a particular project with agreed terms of reference and outputs such as to meet the criteria or terms of the donation or award or grant. The source of restricted funds can be from government, foundations and trusts, grant-awarding bodies, philanthropic organizations, private donations, bequests from wills, etc. A glaring example of misuse of restricted funds would be when Maxwell spent Mirror Group pension funds on Mirror Group development.

Revenue

The total income received in exchange for goods or services during a specific accounting period. Revenue can be recorded using either the cash basis (as received), or the accrual basis (as earned). Also referred to as sales or sales revenue.

'S'

Salaries

Compensation provided by a business to employees, excluding benefits. On an income statement, Salaries refers only to that portion of compensation (such as administrative and management costs) that does not vary in direct proportion to sales. See also labour.

Sales

Another term for Revenue.

Salvage Value

The scrap value of an asset. Acquisition cost minus salvage value yields the total amount that an asset is depreciated over its useful life.

Share capital

The balance sheet nominal value paid into the company by shareholders at the time(s) shares were issued.

Shareholders' funds

A measure of the shareholders' total interest in the company represented by the total share capital plus reserves.

Shareholder Equity

Another term for Equity.

Short-Term Borrowing

Liabilities that represent money borrowed from banks or other institutions to fund the ongoing operations of a business that will come due within one year.

SIC code

The four-digit code prescribed by the Standard Industrial Classification System to categorize businesses according to the types of activities they perform.

Solvency

A company's ability to satisfy its obligations to creditors when they are due. A company is "technically insolvent" if it has enough assets to pay creditors, but cannot liquidate them quickly enough to meet payment deadlines.

Standard Costs

A target or average cost that can be used either to value inventory or as a basis of comparison with actual costs. Standard costs can often be used to calculate cost of sales, in which case standard cost refers to the average amount of materials, direct labour and overhead required to produce a single product or service unit.

Standard Costs Plus Variances

The method of calculating cost of sales that compares the amounts of materials, direct labour and overhead projected in the Cost of Sales assumption (the standard costs) to expenses allocated to the Production department in the Expenses, Property, Plant and Equipment, Payroll and Benefits, and Other Assets Assumptions (the variances).

Statement of Cash Flows

Another term for Cash Flow Statement.

Stockholders' Equity

Another term for Equity.

Straight-Line Method

The simplest form of depreciation, in which an equal expense is recorded in each year of an asset's useful life. For example, if the asset has a purchase price of ₹ 1,200,0000, a useful life of four years and a salvage value of ₹ 200,0000, straight-line depreciation would record ₹ 250,0000 of depreciation each year. See also sum of the years' digits and double-declining balance.

Sum of the Years' Digits (SYD)

A method of recording accelerated depreciation. Also called the sum-of-digits method, it allows the depreciation of an asset based on an inverted scale of the total digits of the asset's useful life. For example, if the useful life is four years, the years' digits (1, 2, 3, and 4) are summed to produce ten, and 4/10ths of the asset's depreciable cost is recognized as an expense the first year, 3/10ths the second year, and so on. See also straight-line method and double-declining balance.

'T'

Tangible Asset

An asset that represents a physical object such as land, furniture, and buildings. Under accounting rules, a tangible asset must have a useful life greater than one year, and must be used in business operations rather than being held for resale. The following types of assets are not considered to be tangible assets: items held for resale, which are considered to be inventory, cash and other liquid assets which are considered as current assets, and abstract assets such as goodwill, which are intangible assets. See also tangible equity.

Tangible Equity

Equity less intangible assets. See the ratios of debt to tangible equity, fixed assets to tangible equity, and return on tangible equity.

Taxes

Levies on the annual income of a business imposed by federal and state governments. On the income statement, this figure does not include property taxes, which are considered an operating expense.

Treasury Stock

Stock that has been reacquired by the company that issued it and is available for retirement or resale. Also called reacquired stock and treasury shares.

Turns

Another term for Inventory Turns.

Typical Collection Pattern

A method used to calculate accounts receivable. This allows you to break down receivables into categories that indicate what percentage of the total is paid within specified lengths of time from the sales date. See also days sales outstanding.

Typical Payment Patter

A method used to calculate accounts payable. It allows the user to break down payables into categories that indicate what percentage of the total is paid within specified lengths of time from the purchase date. See also days payable outstanding.

T/T (telegraphic transfer)

International banking payment method: a telegraphic transfer payment, commonly used/required for import/export trade, between a bank and an overseas party enabling transfer of local or foreign currency by telegraph, cable or telex. Also called a cable transfer. The terminology dates from times when such communications were literally 'wired' – before wireless communications technology.

'U'

Useful Life

An estimate of the period of time over which an asset will be of use to a company. Along with acquisition cost and salvage value, this measure is used to calculate the amount that the asset is depreciated each year.

'V'

Variable Costs

A cost which varies with sales or operational volumes, *e.g.*, materials, fuel, commission payments. Expenditures that change in proportion to increases or decreases in sales or production volumes. See also Fixed Costs.

Variance

The difference between actual and targeted numbers for revenues, expenditures, or productivity. Variances are usually described as either favourable or unfavourable. See also Standard Costs.

'W'

Working Capital

The net amount of current assets and current liabilities. This is equivalent to a company's liquid assets.

Current assets less current liabilities, representing the required investment, continually circulating, to finance stock, debtors, and work in progress.

Z-Score

A bankruptcy predictor based on the formula derived by Dr. Edward Altman. According to the Altman model, a Z-Score of 3.0 or higher indicates that the company is most likely safe based on the financial data; a score below 1.8 means that the firm is probably headed for bankruptcy. In studies, the Z-Score has been shown to have 90% accuracy of prediction of bankruptcy in the first year of the forecast, and 80% accuracy in the second year.

BIBLIOGRAHY

Financial Management

Adams, Peter S. and William A. Harrison: *Essentials of Cash Management*: MD: Treasury Management Association.

Block and Hirt: Foundations of Financial Management; Richard Irwin & Co.

Bowlin, Martin, and Scott.: *Guide to Financial Analysis*; McGraw-Hill.

Brealey, Richard A.: *Principles of Corporate Finance*. NY: McGraw-Hill.

Brigham and Gapenski.: *Financial Management*: Theory and Practice; Dryden Press.

Campsey and Brigham.: *Introduction to Financial Management*, Dryden Press.

Chambers, Donald R. and Nelson R. Lacey.: *"Corporate Ethics and Shareholder Wealth Maximization,"* Financial Practice and Education.

Eiteman, David K., Arthur I. Stonehill, and Michael H. Moffett.: *Multinational Business Finance*. New York: Addison Wesley.

Eun, Cheol S. and Bruce G. Resnick.: *International Financial Management*. New York: Irwin McGraw-Hill.

Gitman, Lawrence J.: *Principles of Managerial Finance*. MA: Addison Wesley Longman.

Hampton.: *Financial Decision Making: Concepts, Problems, and Cases*. Prentice Hall.

Johnson, Hazel.: *Financial Institutions and Markets*: A Global Perspective. NY: McGraw-Hill.

Keown, Arthur, J. William Petty, David F. Scott, Jr. and John D. Martin.: *Foundations of Finance: The Logic and Practice of Financial Management*; Prentice Hall.

Kohler, Heinz.: *Statistics for Business and Economics*. NY: Harper Collins.

Lewellen, Wilbur G., John A. Halloran, and Howard Lanser.: *Financial Management*: An Introduction to Principles and Practice. OH: Southwestern College Pub.

Lowenstein, Roger. When Genius Failed: *The Rise and Fall of Long-Term Capital Management*. Random House.

Martin, Petty, Keown, and Scott.: *Basic Financial Management*; Prentice Hall.

Moyer, Charles R. *Contemporary Financial Management*. OH: Southwestern College Pub.

Petty, Keown, Scott, and Martin. *Basic Financial Management*; Prentice Hall.

Pinches. *Essentials of Financial Management*; Harper & Row.

Ross, Westerfield, and Jordan. *Fundamentals of Corporate Finance*. Irwin.

Schall and Haley. *Introduction to Financial Management*; McGraw-Hill.

Seitz, Neil E. and Mitch Ellison. *Capital Budgeting and Long-term Financing Decisions*. TX: Dryden Press.

Van Horne, James C. and John M. Wachowicz, Jr. *Fundamentals of Financial Management*; Prentice Hall.

Investment Decisions

Accola, W. L. *Assessing risk and uncertainty in new technology investments.* Accounting Horizons.

Ackerman, R. W. ; *Influence of integration and diversity on the investment process.* Administrative Science Quarterly.

Adamany, H. G. and F. A. J. Gonsalves, *Life cycle management*: An integrated approach to managing investments, Journal of Cost Management.

Angelica, R. et al; *Asset mix is the key to investment strategy.* FE: The Magazine for Financial Executives;

Patton M Q; How to use *Qualitative Methods in Evaluation*; California; Sage Publications

Amram, M.; Value Sweep: *Mapping Corporate Growth Opportunities.* Harvard Business School Press.

Arnold, J. H. ; *Assessing capital risk*: You can't be too conservative. Harvard Business Review.

Baker, G. P. *Growth, corporate policies, and the investment opportunity set.* Journal of Accounting and Economics.

Baldenius, T. *Delegated investment decisions and private benefits of control.* The Accounting Review

Bhimani, A., M. Gosselin, K. Soonawalla and M. Ncube; *The value of accounting information in assessing investment risk. Cost Management.*

Bromwich, M. and A. Bhimani; *Strategic investment appraisal. Management Accounting.*

Francis: *Management of Investments.* McGraw-Hill.

Fraser, Lyn M.: *Understanding Financial Statements.* NJ: Prentice Hall.

Gitman, and Joehnk. *Fundamentals of Investing.* Harper & Row.

Hirt, and Block. *Fundamentals of Investment Management.* Irwin.

Jones, Charles P. *Investments: Analysis and Management.* Wiley, John & Sons, Inc.

Ho, S. M. and L. Yang; *Risk perception and handling in capital investment: An empirical study of senior executives in Hong Kong. Advances in Management Accounting.*

Ismail, T. H. and M. Cline; *Investment appraisal under conditions of continuous and discrete cash flows and discounting. Managerial Auditing Journal.*

Kalagnanam, S. and S. K. Schmidt; *Analyzing capital investments in new products. Management Accounting.*

Kite, D.; *Capital budgeting: Integrating environmental impact.* Journal of Cost Management (Summer).

Klammer, T. ; *Improving investment decisions. Management Accounting.*

Kupper, H.; *Investment-based cost accounting as a fundamental basis of decision-oriented management accounting.*

Melicher, Norton. Finance: An *Introduction to Institution, Investment & Management.* OH: Southwester College, Pub.

Lofthouse, Stephen and Jane Raybould. *Investment Management.* Wiley, John & Sons.

Barton, H., Brown, D., Cound, J., Marsh, P., & Willey, K. ; *Does Top Management Add Value to Investment Decisions? Long Range Planning.*

Borcherding, K., Larichev, O. I., & Messick, D. M. (Ed.); *Contemporary Issues in Decision Making.* Amsterdam: North-Holland.

Eisenhardt, K. M., & Zbaracki, M. J. ; *Strategic Decision Making. Strategic Management Journal.*

Freeman, M., & Hobbes, G.; *Capital Budgeting*: Theory vs Practice. Australian Accountant.

Hickson, D. J. (1987). *Decision-making at the Top of Organizations.* Annual Review of Sociology.

Mullen, J. D., & Roth, B. M.; *Decision making*: Its logic and practice. Savage, MD: Rowman & Littlefield.

Myers, S. C.; *Finance Theory and Financial Strategy.* Midland Corporate Finance Journal.

Nutt, P.; *Types of Organizational Decision Processes.* Administrative Science Quarterly.

Peirson, G., Bird, R., Brown, R., & Howard, P.; *Business Finance.* Roseville: McGraw-Hill.

Pennings, J. M. (Ed.). ; Decision Making: *An Organizational Behaviour Approach.* New York: Markus Wiener Publishing.

Pinches, G. E.; *Myopia, Capital Budgeting and Decision Making. Financial Management.*

Rappaport, A.; Creating Shareholder Value: *The New Standard for Business Performance.* New York: Free Press.

Rodrigues, C. A. ; *Improving decision making processes.* San Francisco, CA: Jossey-Bass.

INDEX